Fundamentals of AutoCAD® Using AutoCAD® 2000
Electronics Drafting Workbook

Steven B. Combs
Ivy Tech State College

Jay H. Zirbel
Murray State University

Prentice Hall
Upper Saddle River, New Jersey   Columbus, Ohio

Editor: Stephen Helba
Associate Editor: Michelle Churma
Production Editor: Louise N. Sette
Design Coordinator: Robin G. Chukes
Cover Designer: Brian Deep
Production Manager: Brian Fox
Marketing Manager: Chris Bracken

This book was set in Arial and was printed and bound by Victor Graphics, Inc. The cover was printed by Victor Graphics, Inc.

© 2000 by Prentice-Hall, Inc.
Pearson Education
Upper Saddle River, New Jersey 07458

All rights reserved. No part of this book may be reproduced, in any form or by any means, without permission in writing from the publisher.

Printed in the United States of America

10 9 8 7 6 5 4 3 2 1

ISBN: 0-13-087056-0

Prentice-Hall International (UK) Limited, *London*
Prentice-Hall of Australia Pty. Limited, *Sydney*
Prentice-Hall of Canada, Inc., *Toronto*
Prentice-Hall Hispanoamericana, S. A., *Mexico*
Prentice-Hall of India Private Limited, *New Delhi*
Prentice-Hall of Japan, Inc., *Tokyo*
Prentice-Hall (Singapore) Pte. Ltd., *Singapore*
Editora Prentice-Hall do Brasil, Ltda., *Rio de Janeiro*

Fundamentals of AutoCAD
Electronics Drafting Workbook
Table of Contents

Unit 1: Introduction to AutoCAD and Working with the Windows Environment 1
    Overview 1
    Objectives 1
    Introduction 1
    Section 1: The Basics of Windows for Electronics Users 1
        Creating Project Folders 2
    Section 2: Working with Folders 5
        Creating Electronics Specific Folder and File Names 5
        Adding Files to Project Folders 6
        Using Find to Locate Lost Files 7
    Section 3: Saving a Drawing 8
        Using Sequential File Saves 8
        File Archives and Compression 8
    Unit 1 Review 11
    Unit 1 Assignment #1 13

Unit 2: Creating Your First Drawing 14
    Overview 14
    Objectives 14
    Introduction 14
    Section 1: Setting Up a Drawing 14
        Electronics Units 14
        Setting the Limits for Electronics Paper Sizes 15
    Section 2: Using AutoCAD Drafting Tools 16
        Adjusting the Grid and Snap for Electronics Drawings 16
    Section 3: Drawing Lines 16
        Line Widths in Electronics Drawings 16
    Unit 2 Review 19
    Unit 2 Assignment #1 21
    Unit 2 Assignment #2 23

Unit 3: Viewing and Plotting a Drawing 25
    Overview 25
    Objectives 25
    Introduction 25
    Section 1: Creating Views 25
        Advantages of Using DDVIEW when Creating Electronics Drawings 25
        Creating Multiple Views of Electronics Drawings 26
    Section 2: Introduction to Plotting 29
        Plotting Metric Drawings 29
        Plotting Drawings with Correct Line Widths 29
    Unit 3 Review 31
    Unit 3 Assignment #1 33
    Unit 3 Assignment #2 34

Unit 4: Basic CAD Drawing Techniques 35
    Overview 35
    Objectives 35
    Introduction 35
    Section 1: Setting Display Format and Precision (UNITS and DDUNITS) 35

Angular Measurement...36
　　Tutorial 4.1: Setting Units and Angular Measurement.............................36
　Section 2: Working with Drawing Templates...37
　　Tutorial 4.2: Creating a Metric Drawing Template....................................37
　Section 3: Coordinate System Basics..38
　Unit 4 Review...39
　Unit 4 Assignment #1..41
　Unit 4 Assignment #2..42

Unit 5: Understanding Layers and Linetypes..45
　Overview..45
　Objectives..45
　Introduction..45
　Section 1: Working with Layers..45
　　Naming Layers..45
　　Adding New Layers..46
　　Tutorial 5.1: Creating a Drawing Template with Layers............................46
　　Changing the Layer Color..46
　　Tutorial 5.2: Changing Layer Color..47
　Section 2: Understanding Linetypes..47
　　What Are Linetypes?...48
　　Loading and Setting the Linetype...48
　　Tutorial 5.3: Loading and Setting ISO Linetypes..................................48
　　Understanding Linetype Scale (LTSCALE).......................................49
　Unit 5 Review...51
　Unit 5 Assignment #1..53
　Unit 5 Assignment #2..54

Unit 6: Creating Basic Geometry...55
　Overview..55
　Objectives..55
　Introduction..55
　Drawing Circles (CIRCLE)...55
　　Tutorial 6.1: Beginning the Fuse Symbol...55
　Drawing Arcs (ARC)..56
　　Tutorial 6.2: Creating Arcs with 3 Point and Arc Continue......................57
　Unit 6 Review...59
　Unit 6 Assignment #1..61
　Unit 6 Assignment #2..62

Unit 7: Annotating a Drawing with Text and Hatching...........................63
　Overview..63
　Objectives..63
　Introduction..63
　Section 1: Adding Text to a Drawing..63
　　Selecting the Correct Font..63
　　Defining a Text Style for Electrical Drawings (STYLE).........................64
　　Naming the Text Style..65
　　Selecting the Roman Simplex Font...65
　　Setting the Text Height...65
　　Entering Text and Changing the Style...65
　Section 2: Filling Areas with Hatching..65
　　Defining the Pattern Type...65
　Unit 7 Review...67
　Unit 7 Assignment #1..69
　Unit 7 Assignment #2..69

Unit 7 Assignment #3...70
  Unit 7 Assignment #4...71

Unit 8: Drawing Accurately 73
  Overview 73
  Objectives 73
  Introduction 73
  Section 1: Working with Entity Points and Object Snap...73
      Using Various Object Snaps to Create the Fuse Symbol 74
      QUADrant...74
      ENDpoint..75
      PERpendicular 75
  Unit 8 Review...77
  Unit 8 Assignment #1...79
  Unit 8 Assignment #2...80
  Unit 8 Assignment #3...81

Unit 9: Creating Selection Sets...82
  Overview 82
  Objective 82
  Introduction 82
  Section 1: Methods for Creating Selection Sets...82
      The GROUP Command 82
  Unit 9 Review...87
  Unit 9 Assignment #1...89

Unit 10: Basic Editing Skills..91
  Overview 91
  Objectives 91
  Introduction 91
  Section 1: Offsetting, Rotating, Mirroring, Scaling, and Stretching Objects 91
      Using Various Editing Commands to Create Electronics Parts 91
      OFFSET 91
      ROTATE...93
      STRETCH 93
      MIRROR...93
      SCALE..93
  Section 2: Editing Edges and Corners of Objects 93
      The FILLET Command...93
      The CHAMFER Command 94
  Section 3: Producing Arrays of Objects..94
      Using Rectangular Arrays to Create a Schematic Representation of an External
      Thread..94
      Using Polar Arrays to Create Equidistant Holes 94
  Unit 10 Review...95
  Unit 10 Assignment #1...97
  Unit 10 Assignment #2...99

Unit 11: Editing With Grips...101
  Overview 101
  Objective 101
  Introduction 101
  Section 1: Working with Grips 101
      Using Grips to Assist in the Creation of Electronics Drawings 101
      Stretch 101
      Move...102

v

  Rotate 102
  Scale 102
  Mirror 102
 Unit 11 Review 103
 Unit 11 Assignment #1 105
 Unit 11 Assignment #2 107

Unit 12: Advanced Drawing Techniques 109
 Overview 109
 Objectives 109
 Introduction 109
 Section 1: Working with POINT and MEASURE to Create a Resistor Symbol 109
  Setting the Point Style and Size 110
  Using MEASURE to Create the Resistor Symbol 110
 Section 2: Creating IC Pads with DONUT 112
 Section 3: Creating Symbols and PCBs with Polylines 113
  Creating a Diode Symbol with Polylines 114
  Turning Fill ON and OFF 115
 Unit 12 Review 117
 Unit 12 Assignment #1 119
 Unit 12 Assignment #2 121

Unit 13: Dimensioning a Drawing 123
 Overview 123
 Introduction 123
 Section 1: Dimensioning Basics 123
  ASME Standards 123
  Creating Dimension Styles 124
  United States (US) Customary 124
  International System of Units (SI) 128
 Section 2: Linear and Radial Dimensioning 130
  Linear Dimensions 130
  Aligned Dimensions 130
  Radial Dimensioning 130
 Unit 13 Review 131
 Unit 13 Assignment #1 133
 Unit 13 Assignment #2 135

Unit 14: Modifying Object Characteristics and Extracting Information
from your Drawing 137
 Overview 137
 Objectives 137
 Introduction 137
 Section 1: Modifying Object Properties 137
  Moving an Object to a Different Layer 138
 Section 2: Editing a Polyline with PEDIT 139
  Using PEDIT to Create a Spline Curve 140
 Unit 14 Review 141
 Unit 14 Assignment #1 143

Unit 15: Using Symbols and Attributes 145
 Overview 145
 Objectives 145
 Introduction 145
 Section 1: Creating and Inserting a Block of the Resistor Symbol 145
  Creating a Block of a Resistor Symbol 145

Inserting the Resistor Symbol into a Drawing 147
Section 2: Adding Information to a Resistor Symbol with Attributes 148
Creating the Resistor Symbol 148
Defining the Resistor Attributes 149
Creating a Block of the Resistor and Attributes 150
Inserting the Block of the Resistor and Attributes 150
Unit 15 Review...151
Unit 15 Assignment #1...153

Unit 16: Creating Isometric Drawings 163
Overview..163
Objectives 163
Introduction 163
Section 1: Understanding Isometric and Pictorial Drawings 164
Isometric Detail Drawings 164
Isometric Exploded Assembly Drawings 166
Unit 16 Review...169
Unit 16 Assignment #1...171
Unit 16 Assignment #2...173

Unit 1: Introduction to AutoCAD and Working with the Windows Environment

Overview

In the textbook that this workbook accompanies, AutoCAD and the Windows environment were introduced. In this supplement, features of AutoCAD and Windows that will assist the mechanical drafter/designer in becoming a more efficient user will be presented.

In general, AutoCAD is not the only tool that is used by a electronics drafter/designer. There are many occasions when a word processor is used to prepare memos, a spreadsheet to prepare a project budget, and presentation software to prepare sales or design presentations. The Windows environment allows the creation of folders that will group the shortcuts to the software and the files needed to complete a project. As projects are created and completed, it will be necessary to save and archive files for later editing.

Objectives

- Create project folders.
- Create electronics specific folders.
- Creating file shortcuts to project folders.
- Use find to locate lost files.
- Create sequential files.
- Understand file archiving and compression.

Introduction

Using AutoCAD to create electronics drawings can be a very rewarding and enjoyable experience. But, in order to make the experience pleasant, there is a fair amount of preparation that should be done to avoid such frustrations as lost and corrupt files. Although lost files are not "show stoppers," it is very frustrating and time consuming to locate them. On the other hand, corrupt files can be the source of many hours of lost work. When used together, AutoCAD and Windows provide efficient tools to ensure that these frustrations are minimized.

Section 1: The Basics of Windows for Electronics Users

There are many occasions when it may be required to use other software to complete a project. It may be necessary to insert an AutoCAD drawing into a word processing document or electronic presentation. A bill of materials may need to be created in a spreadsheet so that the total cost of the parts can be quickly calculated and then inserted into the AutoCAD drawing. While this section does not describe the procedures for these tasks, it will show how to group computer application shortcuts into a folder so that immediate access is available to all applications required to complete a project.

Creating Project Folders

One of the most unused features of Windows is the desktop. The desktop, as described in the main text, is the area that appears on the screen when Windows is started. A typical desktop is shown in figure 1.1.

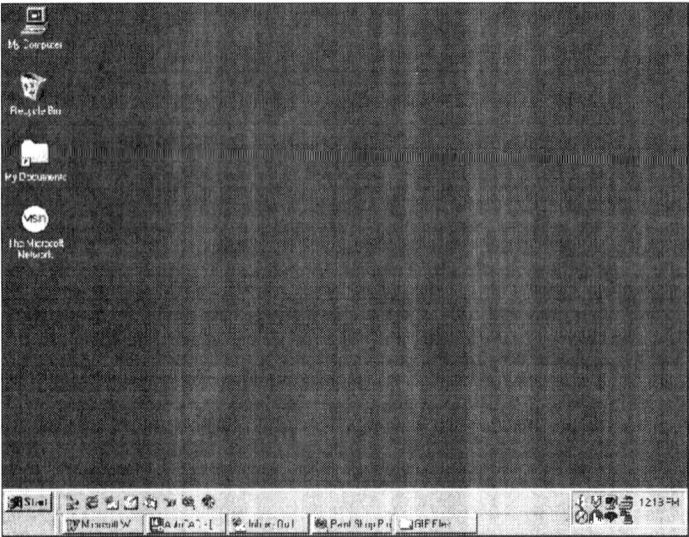

Figure 1.1 *A typical electronic draftsman's Windows desktop.*

The desktop is a great place to create project folders. Project folders allow files to be grouped for quick access. The creation of project folders is very easy. Follow these steps for creating a project folder on the desktop.

1. Ensure that the Windows desktop is displayed as shown in figure 1.1.

2. Place the cursor anywhere on the desktop except on top of an icon.

3. Click the right mouse button once. A menu will appear as shown in figure 1.2.

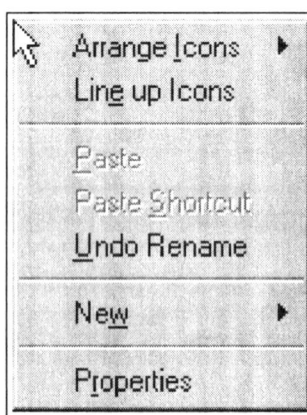

Figure 1.2 *Clicking the right mouse button on the desktop causes this menu to appear.*

4. Move the cursor to the New selection. Another menu will appear as shown in figure 1.3.

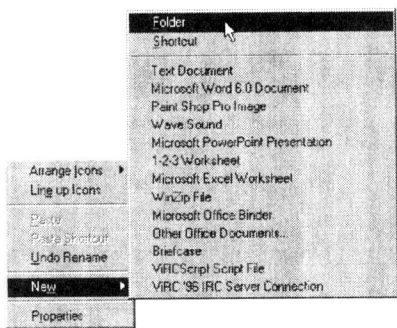

Figure 1.3 *The New flyout menu.*

5. Move the cursor to the Folder option and click the left mouse button to select that option. A new folder will appear on the desktop as shown in figure 1.4. The *New Folder* default name will be highlighted. This name should be changed to the name of the project that will be contained within this folder.

Figure 1.4 *This New Folder icon will appear when the New Folder option is selected.*

6. With the New Folder name highlighted, enter the new name for the project and press `Enter`. The name will change as shown in figure 1.5. The project file has now been created.

Figure 1.5 *The named project folder.*

Once the folder has been named, determine which computer applications will be necessary to complete the project. For this example, AutoCAD and Microsoft Excel, an electronic spreadsheet, will be necessary to complete our project.

3

> **SKILL BUILDER**
>
> Don't worry if you are unsure which applications are necessary at the beginning of a project. It is very easy to add application shortcuts at a later time, as they are needed.

The complete application is not stored in this folder, only the shortcut to the application's *executable file*. The executable file is simply the file that starts the application. The shortcut is a pointer to the location of that file. Executable files usually have the *.exe* file extension. While locating this file may at first sound like a daunting task, Windows has already done so upon installation of the application. When most applications are installed Windows places a shortcut on the taskbar. Copy the shortcut to the project file using the following method if a shortcut to the application is found on the taskbar.

1. Move the cursor to the Start button on the taskbar.

2. Right-click on the Start button. A menu will appear.

3. Select the Explore option. The Windows Explorer will be started as shown in figure 1.6. The Windows Explorer is a file management tool that is included with Windows to allow easy file management. This tool has many functions and features. Consult a Windows manual for more information on its use. On the right-hand side of the Windows Explorer window are all of the folders that are contained on the taskbar.

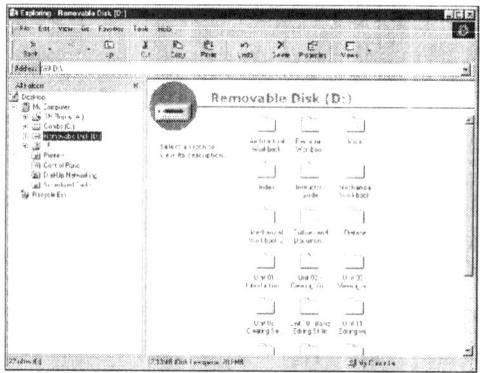

Figure 1.6 *The Windows Explorer.*

4. Double-click the folder that contains the application's shortcut.

5. Once the application's shortcut icon is found, single-click the icon.

6. Select Edit Copy from the Windows Explorer pulldown menu. The shortcut is copied to the clipboard. The clipboard is a temporary storage location and is used to allow for easy exchange of information between applications.

7. Close Windows Explorer. The desktop should be displayed.

8. Double-click the project folder. The folder will open. Notice that there are no application shortcuts for files.

9. Select Edit Paste from the project file's window pulldown menu. The shortcut copied will appear in the project window as shown in figure 1.7. The application's shortcut icon has a curved arrow on the bottom left. This arrow indicates that a shortcut, and not the actual file, has been copied.

Figure 1.7 *The project window with an application shortcut.*

SKILL BUILDER

If an application shortcut cannot be found on the taskbar, it does not mean that the application has not been installed: it simply means that a shortcut has not been created. To create a shortcut, locate the executable file. Refer to the software's documentation for more information.

Section 2: Working with Folders

Once a project folder has been created and shortcuts to applications have been created, it is time to get to work. As mentioned in the main text, it is important to store files in folders with proper naming conventions for both the folders and files. Once these files are saved in folders, then shortcuts to these files can be created in a project folder on the desktop for easy access. If you do not use the desktop and proper naming techniques, it may be necessary to use the Find function within Windows to locate a file. This is an extra step that takes time away from drawing and designing.

Creating Electronics Specific Folder and File Names

With 256 characters and spaces, Windows allows very descriptive file names. Make use of this feature. It can save time. However, do not overdo it! Too many characters will clutter the windows and crowd icons. An example of a typical project may help the explanation.

A electronics firm is creating a set of working drawings for a new widget. The widget contains 6 different components on three C-size sheets; one sheet contains two of the six parts, one sheet contains the other four parts, and the last sheet contains an assembly drawing as well as the bill of materials. The draftsperson might use the folder names and file names shown in figure 1.8.

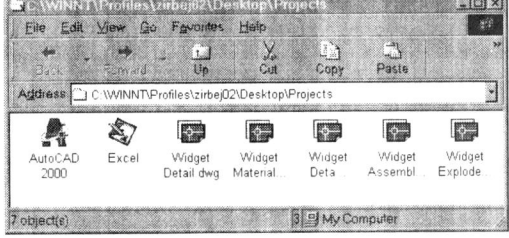

Figure 1.8 *A sample project window for the widget working drawings.*

By using descriptive folder names and file names, anyone in the electronics firm can locate the files quickly for later viewing or editing. Dates in file names are not necessary as they can be displayed using the Details View as shown in figure 1.9. To choose the Details View select View Details from the folder window's pulldown menu. The dates and times shown in the Details View indicate the last date and time the file was modified.

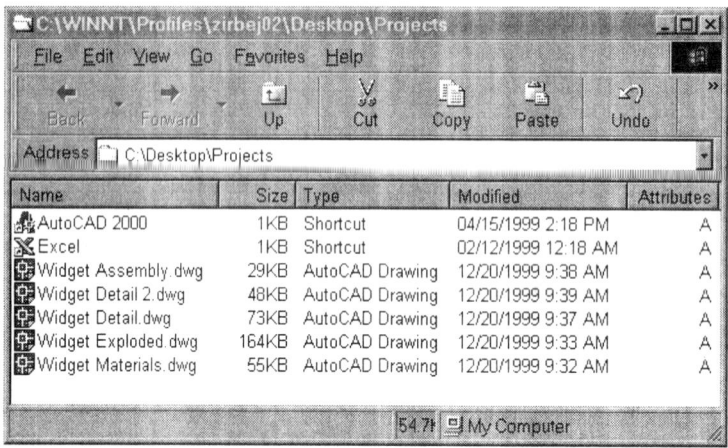

Figure 1.9 *Displaying the file names in the Details View.*

Folders can be created on a storage device (hard drive, floppy, etc.) or on the desktop as described in the example project folder above.

Adding Files to Project Folders

Once a file has been created and saved to a storage device, a shortcut to that file may be added in the project folder as well. By including this file in the project folder, not only are the applications used to complete a project listed, but also the files. This is also handy if the project files themselves are located in various folders on a storage device. The project folder consolidates the files in a single location without affecting their actual storage location. To copy a file shortcut to a project window, use the following procedure:

1. Ensure that the desktop is displayed.

2. Double-click on the *My Computer* Icon. A window that contains all storage devices will be displayed.

3. Continue working through the storage devices until the file to be included as a shortcut in the project folder is found.

4. Open the project folder.

5. Move the two folders if necessary so that both can be viewed on the desktop.

6. Using the right button drag the file from its storage device location to the project folder.

7. Release the button when the file icon is located in the project folder. A menu will appear.

8. Select the Create Shortcut(s) Here option. A shortcut icon for the file will be created in the project folder.

9. Close both windows.

Once the project folder has been created, and applications and files have been created within the folder, there is no longer a need to search the taskbars and storage devices for the applications and files. They are now conveniently on the desktop and may remain there until the project is completed. To continue working on the project, double-click one of the files in the project folder. The file and the application used to create the file will automatically be loaded.

Using Find to Locate Lost Files

There are occasions when certain drawing files cannot be located. AutoCAD provides a search function that allows files to be found, but with its many options it can be very intimidating to use. A quick and easy method of locating drawing files is to use the built-in Windows Find feature. Located on the taskbar, Find will search for files, folders, or computers on a network. Selecting the Files or Folders... option will display the Find: Files window as shown in figure 1.10.

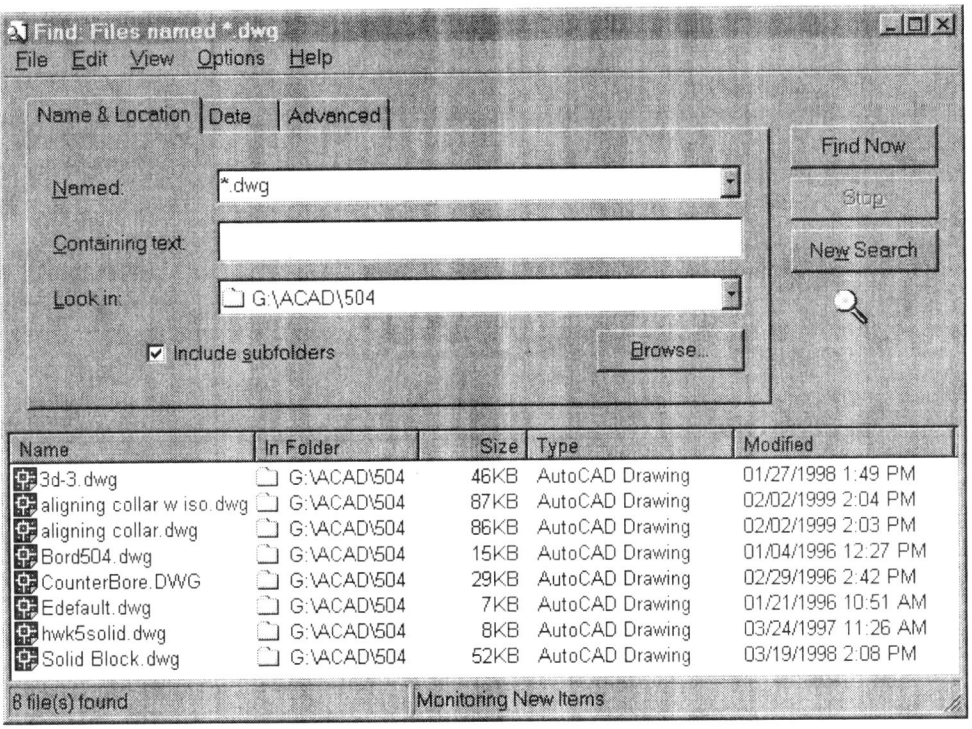

Figure 1.10 *The Find Window.*

If *.dwg (all AutoCAD files have this extension) is entered in the Named text edit box, select the appropriate storage device, and select Find Now. Windows will locate every file with the .dwg extension as shown in figure 1.10.

Section 3: Saving a Drawing

As mentioned in the main text, there are many commands that save drawing files. Electronics draftsmen/designers must save drawings frequently and make constant backups. One technique that decreases the likelihood of lost files is to use a method known as Sequential File Saves.

Using Sequential File Saves

Sequential File Saves (SFS) is a method whereby files are saved in numerical and chronological order. As any good CAD operator knows, files should be saved regularly during their creation and modifications. Just how often depends on the amount of time the CAD operator is willing to lose. But a good CAD operator should also save multiple copies of drawings at various stages. This procedure offers two advantages:

1. A drawing can be retrieved at various stages during its development for further experimentation.

2. If the present file being modified happens to become corrupt (unusable) then a backup file from a previous stage can be reloaded and the object can be recreated.

An example of utilization of SFS can be found in the following example. A file, *My Drawing.dwg,* is being created. During the first hour of work, the CAD operator issues a QSAVE every 15 minutes. After the first hour the CAD operator executes the SAVEAS command. The CAD operator saves the file as *My Drawing(01).dwg*. There are now two files. *My Drawing.dwg* contains the first hour of work, and *My Drawing(01).dwg* contains the next hour of work. The CAD operator will continue doing this until the project is complete. If storage space becomes low, the CAD operator can determine the need for retaining previous versions of the project and delete them accordingly.

File Archives and Compression

Once a project is complete, it is generally not needed again unless new hard copies are needed or a change in the initial design is needed before the drawings are used again. These unused files and projects can take up valuable space on storage devices. When the files are no longer being used on a regular basis, they should be considered for *archival*. Archival simply means that the file will be moved from a primary storage device onto a floppy, tape, removable hard drive, or other device. Once archived, the file can be stored in a separate and safe location such as a vault or lock box. This allows for added security of critical files from damage and theft.

To further save space on the archival storage media, *compression* may be used. Compression is a technique for making files size smaller. Once files are compressed, they cannot be used again until they are *decompressed*. A typical AutoCAD drawing can be compressed by as much as 75%. Another advantage of compression is that multiple files may be compressed within a single file. This allows all files of a project to be stored in one small file. Popular compression software for Windows is WinZip. Using the drag and drop technology of Windows, files can be compressed and decompressed with ease. A sample of the interface and a project file that has been compressed is shown in figure 1.11.

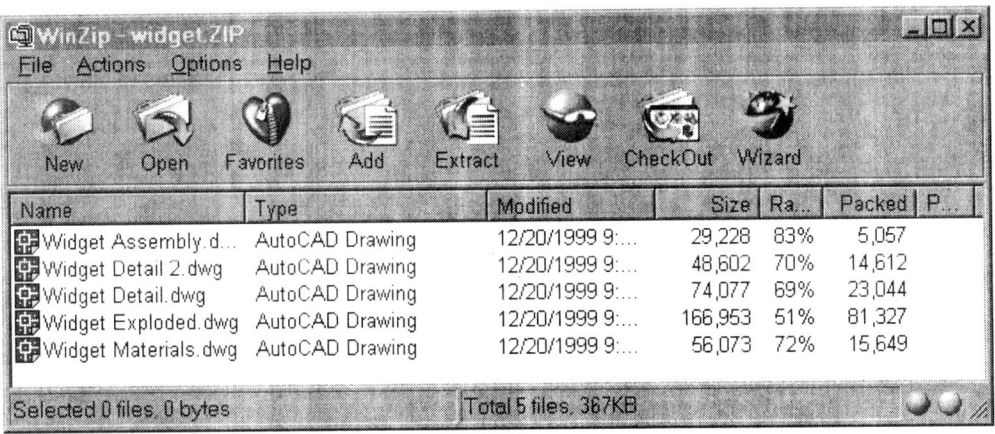

Figure 1.11 *The WinZip compression software.*

NAME _____

Unit 1 Review

1. _Win 98/XP etc._ is an operating system that is necessary to run the Windows version of AutoCAD.

2. The _Command_ _prompt_ is used to issue commands via the keyboard.

3. _Pulldown Menus_ and _Toolbars_ are used to issue commands with the mouse.

4. In Windows, _Folders_ are used to group files on a storage device.

5. The _New_ command allows the utilization of a prototype file.

6. The _Open_ command allows a drawing to be loaded in Read-Only mode.

7. The _QSAVE_ command saves a drawing file without displaying a dialog box.

8. The technique for storing frequently used files is known as _Sequential File Saving_

9. To make files smaller and conserve space, _compression_ is used.

10. The _Quit_ command is used to close AutoCAD without saving the current drawing.

Unit 1 Assignment #1

Read the following scenario:

Widgets by Gidget have just hired you as a draftsperson for a prominent electronics engineering firm. Based on your AutoCAD and computer skills you have been asked to work with the senior electronics engineer, Mrs. Roland, in developing a new personal digital assistant (PDA) known as the Lizard. You have been asked to design the casing for the PDA. The casing will be composed of four separate parts; the top, the bottom, the screen cover, and the battery compartment cover. This job is being contracted from the developer, Pear Tree Computers, and the mold is the only design required. Mrs. Roland informs you that the two of you will have to complete the following tasks for the project:

- Create a complete set of working drawings that show the assembly of the case with the electronics circuitry.
- Prepare progress documents for the developer.
- Prepare a formal presentation to the developer.
- Prepare a manufacturing cost statement.

Using the above information, complete the following tasks:

1. Format a floppy disk.

2. On the floppy disk, create a folder with an appropriate name that will contain the project.

3. Create shortcuts for all of the applications that will be required to complete the assignment.

4. Create several AutoCAD files on the floppy that represent the drawings that have to be created. Use appropriate naming conventions. The files do not need to contain any information. Empty files will do.

5. Ensure that the project window is in Details View.

(Alternative Assignment)

Using the same assignment, list the steps necessary to complete the requirements on paper. Make sure that you list the names for the project folder and the files.

Unit 2: Creating Your First Drawing

Overview

There are many instances where the commands discussed in the main text have general settings and uses. In this unit specific commands and features are introduced that will assist in the creation of electronic drawings. Many of the commands simulate the tools used when creating manual drawings. For those that have never created a manual drawing, they will find that AutoCAD includes any command needed to create accurate and precise electronic drawings.

Objectives

- Establish units for English and metric drawings.
- List the various electronic paper sizes.
- Use the grid and snap to assist in the creation of electronic drawings.
- Establish and create proper line widths.

Introduction

There are many standards to conform to when creating electronic drawings. In manual drafting we often have to determine an appropriate scale for the drawing, select the proper paper size, and ensure proper line width and quality. While AutoCAD will automate some tasks, there are others where human decisions must be made. It is important to know what the standards are to ensure accurate and correct electronic drawings. This unit will introduce some of those standards and how to obtain the best results.

Section 1: Setting up a Drawing

Drawing setup is the first step in creating an electronic drawing. During this phase of drawing creation, the drafter must make decisions concerning the scale of the drawing and the selection of a proper sheet size. These two factors must be considered together to create a drawing that is large enough to be easily read by the manufacturer. AutoCAD has two commands that make this decision much easier.

Electronics Units

When creating an electronic drawing, two different units of measure may be utilized: United States (US) Customary, and International System (SI) of Units. US Customary units, or inches, are usually expressed as decimal units and the precision, or number of decimal places, is dependent upon the precision needed during the manufacturing process. SI units, or millimeters (mm), are usually expressed as decimal units with a precision of zero decimal places unless very tight precision is needed during the manufacturing process. When creating an electronic drawing, determine the type of units necessary. For both types of measurements, Decimal Units are selected in the Units Control dialog box. For SI units, select a precision of 0. For US Customary units, select a precision equal to the tightest precision necessary. For example, if a part is to be manufactured and the precision is to the nearest sixteenth of an inch (.0625), choose a precision of 0.0000. If a part is to be manufactured and the precision is to the nearest quarter of an inch (.25), choose a precision of 0.00.

Setting the Limits for Electronics Paper Sizes

There are various sizes of paper that can be used when creating an electronic drawing. Table 2.1 lists the common sheet sizes in both inches and millimeters as identified by the American Society of Mechanical Engineers (ASME). The sizes shown are in landscape orientation. That is, they are wider than they are tall. For portrait orientation, taller than they are wide, reverse the numbers for each sheet size.

Sheet Size	Outside Limit (in)	Outside Limit (mm)	Suggested Drawing Area (in)	Suggested Drawing Area (mm)
A	11 X 8.5		9 X 7	230 X 170
B	11 X 17		15 X 10	380 X 250
C	22 X 17		20 X 15	500 X 380
D	34 X 22		32 X 20	800 X 500
E	44 X 34		42 X 32	1060 X 800
F	40 X 28		38 X 26	950 X 650

Table 2.1 *Sheet sizes in inches and the suggested drawing area in inches and millimeters (landscape orientation).*

When establishing units for your drawing, you should consider setting the upper right limits, using LIMMAX, to the suggested drawing area shown in table 2.1. This will leave a half-inch margin around the edge of the actual paper size. If you are creating a metric drawing, multiply values by 25.4 and round to the nearest millimeter. Compute these values and place them in Table 2.1 for future reference. You will find that these values work well with plotters, but they may not work with printer technology. Unit 3 - Viewing and Plotting a Drawing will discuss this matter in further detail.

When creating drawings in AutoCAD, always be sure to create the object at full scale or true dimensions. Never divide the dimensions by two to create a drawing that will be plotted at half scale. This technique leads to numerous errors and, as you will find later in the text, can cause serious problems when applying dimensions to a drawing. To create a drawing that will be plotted at half scale, multiply the limits by two. To create a drawing that will be plotted at quarter scale, multiply the limits by four. To create a drawing that will be plotted at double scale, multiply the limits by two. The appropriate adjustments will be made when plotting to ensure that the hardcopy, or plotted piece of paper, is to scale.

Section 2: Using AutoCAD Drafting Tools

The most fundamental AutoCAD drafting tools include the grid and snap. The grid and snap assists in ensuring lines are drawn precisely and accurately. Although grid and snap settings are typically personal preferences, there are a few tips and tricks that will ensure they are used more effectively when creating electronic drawings.

Adjusting the Grid and Snap for Electronics Drawings

Consider the following when utilizing grid and snap for electronic drawings. Remember that these are only guidelines and it may be necessary to use other values or even change the values while creating a drawing.

For US Customary drawings:

- Find the most common divisor for the dimensions of the part being drawn. For instance, dimensions of 1, .5, .25, and .125 are all divisible by .125. In this instance, .125 would be a good starting point for the snap setting.
- Once a snap setting has been determined, double the value for the grid setting. If the grid is too dense, quadruple the setting.

For SI drawings:

- Set the snap to 1 for small drawings since most dimensions are rounded up to the nearest millimeter. Set the snap to 2 for larger drawings.
- Set the grid to 5 or 10 accordingly.

For both systems:

- Don't be afraid to change the snap and grid settings. There are situations where it is advantageous to change the grid and snap temporarily to assist in the creation of small or intricate parts.
- Don't forget to turn snap on and verify that snap is activated using the coordinates display.

Section 3: Drawing Lines

When creating manual drawings, a big concern is that proper line widths are used to distinguish among various linetypes and that the quality of the line is such that a good copy of the print may be obtained from the original.

Line Widths in Electronics Drawings

There are four common line widths that are used when creating technical drawings. Table 2.2 lists these widths and their use.

Line Width	Use(s)
.3	Center Lines, Dimension Lines, Leader Lines, and Boundary Lines
.5	Text
.7	Object, Connection, and Shielding
.9	Border

Table 2.2 *Common line widths and uses.*

AutoCAD allows you to control what you see on the screen and print with *lineweights*. Lineweights can be controlled by layer, or by individual object. You can toggle the display and plotting of lineweights on and off in the Status Bar with the LWT button.

The *lineweight* option will be discussed in later units. For now, use the default line width and concentrate on learning how to begin drawings and create basic shapes. Once you are comfortable with these techniques and the other units have been presented, consider trying your hand at varying line widths.

NAME _____

Unit 2 Review

1. The common units of measure for an electronic drawing are English and _Metrics_.

2. The measurements for an A-size sheet of paper are __11__ x __8.5__ inches.

3. The __GRID__ command creates a series of dots on the drawing area that act as visual cues to specific distances.

4. __Ortho__ mode is used to ensure that only horizontal or vertical lines are created.

5. Hidden lines are usually created with a line thickness of __.3__ mm.

6. Object lines are usually created with a line thickness of __.7__ mm.

7. When creating drawings in AutoCAD, always be sure to create the object at __Full__ scale or true dimensions.

8. The __DDRMODES__ command will display the Drawing Aids dialog box.

9. The measurements for a C-size sheet of paper are __24__ x __34__ mm.

10. The quickest way to "clean up" the drawing area is to use the __Redraw__ command.

19

Unit 2 Assignment #1

In this assignment you will create the top, front, and right orthographic views of the Angle Block as shown in figure 2.1.

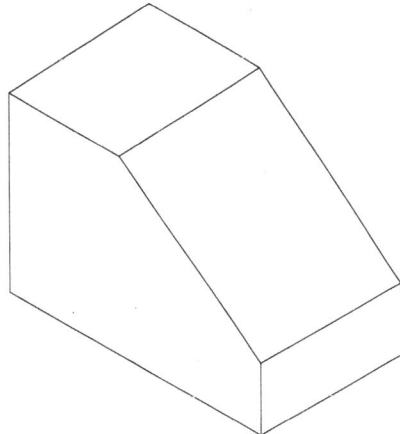

Figure 2.1 *An isometric view of the Angle Block.*

Follow the steps below to assist you in creating this drawing.

1. Create a new drawing called *Angle Block*.

2. Set units to decimal with a precision of 0.000.

3. Set upper right limits to 10.5,8. This will set up the drawing to fit on an A-size sheet of paper.

4. Set the grid to .5 units. This setting will match the grid shown on the next page and allow you to easily identify distances for lines and spacing of the views.

5. Set the snap to .25.

6. Since the majority of the lines in this drawing are horizontal and vertical, you may wish to invoke ortho mode.

7. Create a border around the limits of the drawing.

8. Re-create the drawing using the LINE command to create all objects. Be sure to use the grid shown and the snap function to assist in the creation of the objects. Note that some endpoints do not fall on grid points, but between them.

9. Use the QSAVE command often.

10. When complete, use the END command and save the drawing to the device you or your instructor chooses.

11. You will plot these drawings in the next unit. Be sure to safeguard the device where your files are stored.

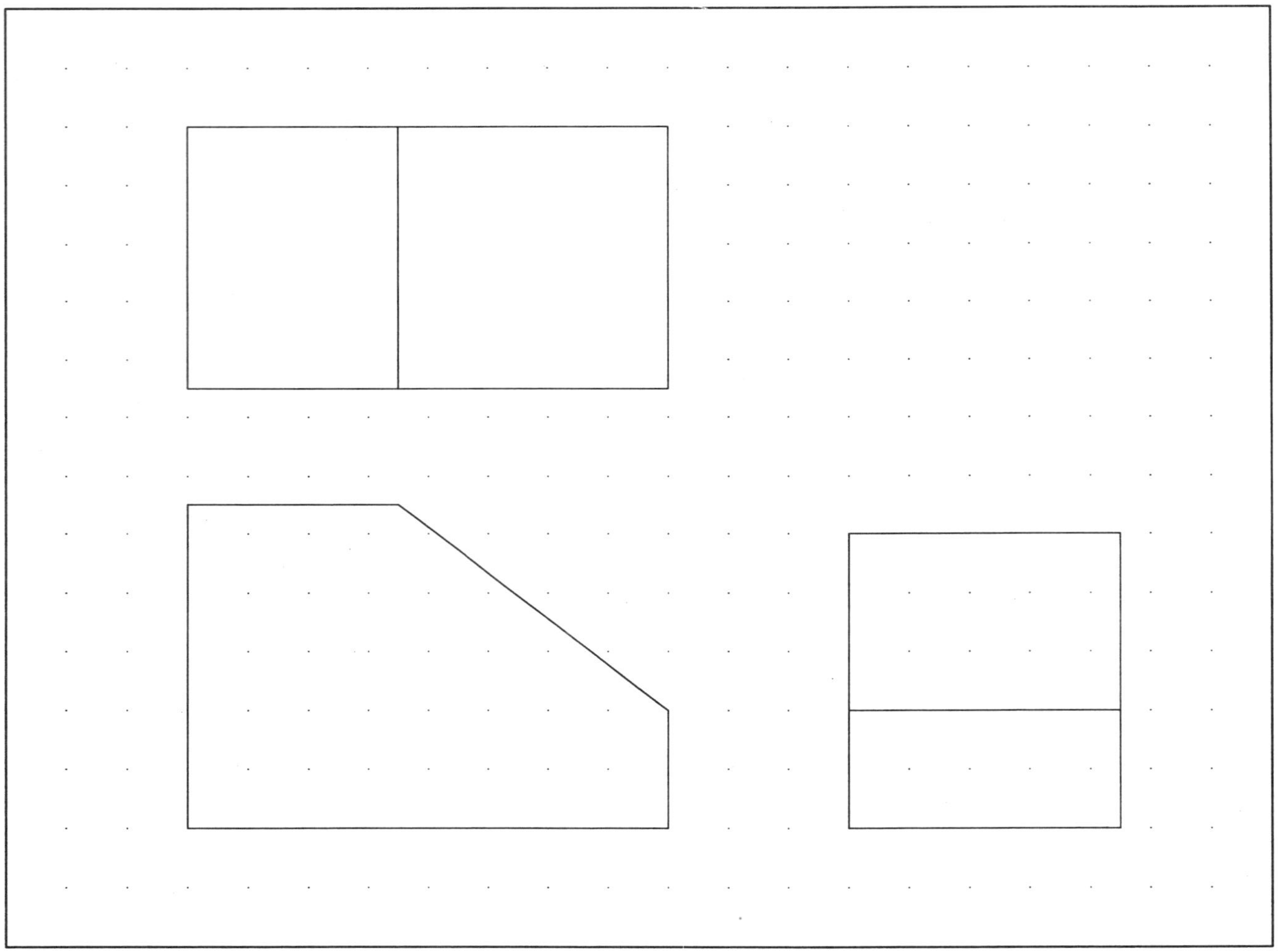

Figure 2.2 *The orthographic view of the Angle Block.*

22

Unit 2 Assignment #2

In this assignment you will create a drawing of the block diagram found on the following page. Follow the steps below to assist you in creating this drawing.

1. Create a new drawing called *Block Diagram*.

2. Set units to decimal with a precision of 0.000.

3. Set upper right limits to 10.5,8. This will set up the drawing to fit on an A-size sheet of paper.

4. Set the grid to .5 units. This setting will match the grid shown on the next page and allow you to easily identify distances for lines and spacing of the views.

5. Set the snap to .25.

6. Since all of the lines in this drawing are horizontal and vertical, you may wish to invoke ortho mode.

7. Create a border around the limits of the drawing.

8. Re-create the drawing shown on the next page using the LINE command to create all objects. Be sure to use the grid shown and the snap function to assist in the creation of the objects. Note that some endpoints do not fall on grid points, but between them. You are not required to add the text to this drawing at this time.

9. Use the QSAVE command often.

10. When the drawing is complete, use the END command and save it to the device you or your instructor chooses.

11. You will plot these drawings in the next unit. Be sure to safeguard the device where your files are stored.

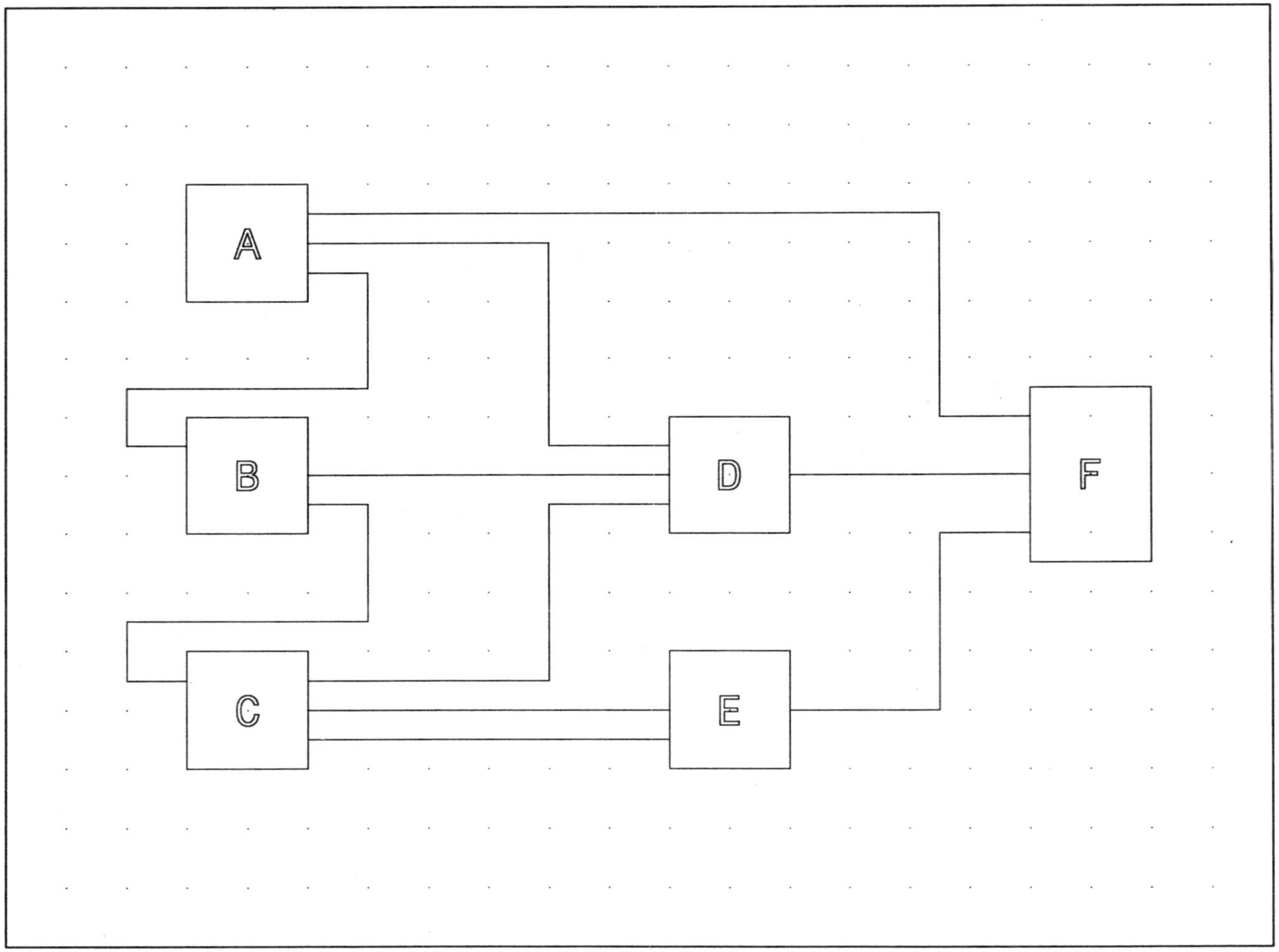

Figure 2.3 *The Block Diagram drawing.*

Unit 3: Viewing and Plotting a Drawing

Overview

The main text explained that viewing and plotting were very important skills necessary to create a drawing, as well as maintaining a record of the drawing using hardcopy. There are various commands and features in AutoCAD that allow the electronic draftsperson to become more efficient and productive. Various paper sizes used in the electronic field were introduced in the last unit. In this unit, we explain how to create hardcopy of your electronic drawing on standard sheet sizes. Plotting metric drawings will also be discussed in more detail. The assignments at the end of this unit will test your knowledge and skill in plotting several drawings with different scale factors.

Objectives

- Understand the advantages of saving views in an electronics drawing.
- Utilize and understand the creation of multiple viewports.
- Understand how to plot electronic drawings with correct line widths.
- Understand the steps necessary to properly plot a metric drawing.

Introduction

This unit will introduce more commands that will assist you in creating and plotting electronic drawings. Do not become overwhelmed with the number of commands being introduced. Make note of them and then try to use them when appropriate. After time, commands such as VPORTS will become part of the everyday AutoCAD routine. These commands can significantly enhance drawing productivity.

Metric drawings have always been a mystery to new engineering, design, and drafting students. While there have been many attempts to ensure that industry understands this measuring system, many are still resistant to change. This unit will introduce the metric system in more detail and explain some of the advantages available when incorporating this system into electronic drawings.

Section 1: Creating Views

Just as in other units, it is often advantageous to learn how certain commands can be applied to electronic drawings. The DDVIEW command is no exception. This section will discuss those advantages and will also introduce the concepts of viewports.

Advantages of Using DDVIEW when Creating Electronics Drawings

When creating electronic drawings, especially those that are large and complicated, a lot of productive hours could be lost zooming and panning in on specific portions of the drawings to make corrections and modifications. What if a single sheet of a working drawing contained over 10 different areas of detail? It would be a definite advantage to have views saved of each of those areas so that if and when the drawing had to be modified, the draftsperson could simply restore the view of the section.

Once views are created, it is a simple matter of restoring them in order to modify the individual detail drawings. This will also make it easier for someone else to modify the drawing. That person can simply use the VIEW command, note the saved named views in the View dialog box (figure 3.1), and restore the one that needs further work.

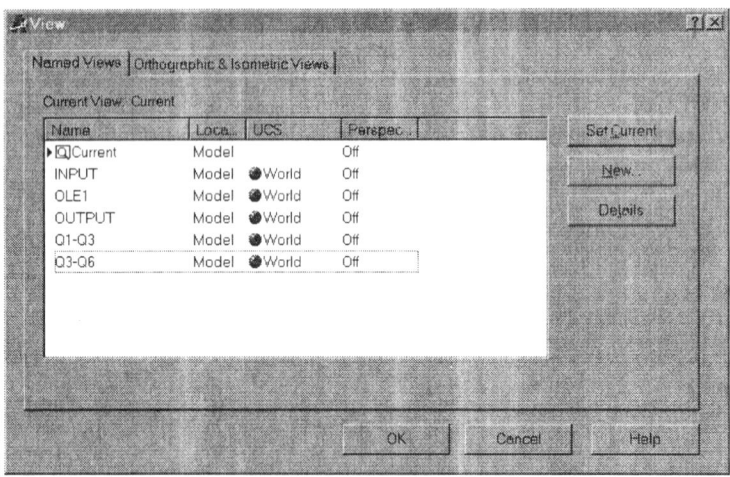

Figure 3.1 *The View dialog box that contains various saved views.*

Descriptive names should be used when views are saved. Avoid using a vague numbering system to name views.

SKILL BUILDER

Plotting saved views is an option in the Plot dialog box. It is handy to have views saved to limit the amount of information to be placed on hardcopy.

Creating Multiple Views of Electronics Drawings

Once you have created and saved views of various portions of a drawing, it is helpful to be able to display more than one of these views within the AutoCAD drawing area at one time. The VPORTS command allows just that. Using this command, the AutoCAD drawing area can be sectioned into more than one viewport. Figure 3.2 shows the AutoCAD drawing area sectioned into 3 different views.

- Select View/Viewports from the pulldown menu.
- Enter VPORTS at the command prompt.

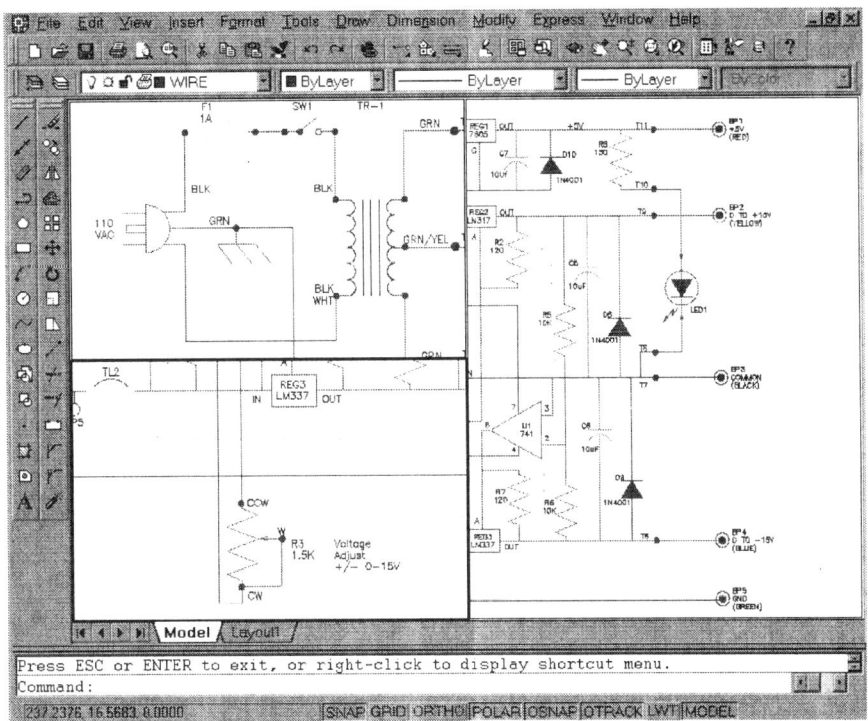

Figure 3.2 *Use the VPORTS command to create multiple viewports of an AM radio circuit drawing.*

If you use the pulldown menus you will be presented with the pulldown menu shown in figure 3.3. The options available in the Viewports menu described below.

- **Named Viewports...** When selected the Viewports dialog box appears as shown in figure 3.4, but with the Named Viewports tab selected. Use this dialog box to select a previously saved named viewport configuration
- **New Viewports...** Accesses the Viewports dialog box appears as shown in figure 3.4 with the New Viewports tab selected. Use this dialog box to select the viewport configuration desired. You can also name a viewport configuration by entering the name in the New name: text box.

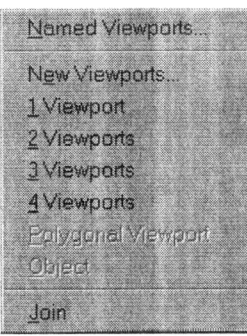

Figure 3.3 *The Viewports pulldown menu options.*

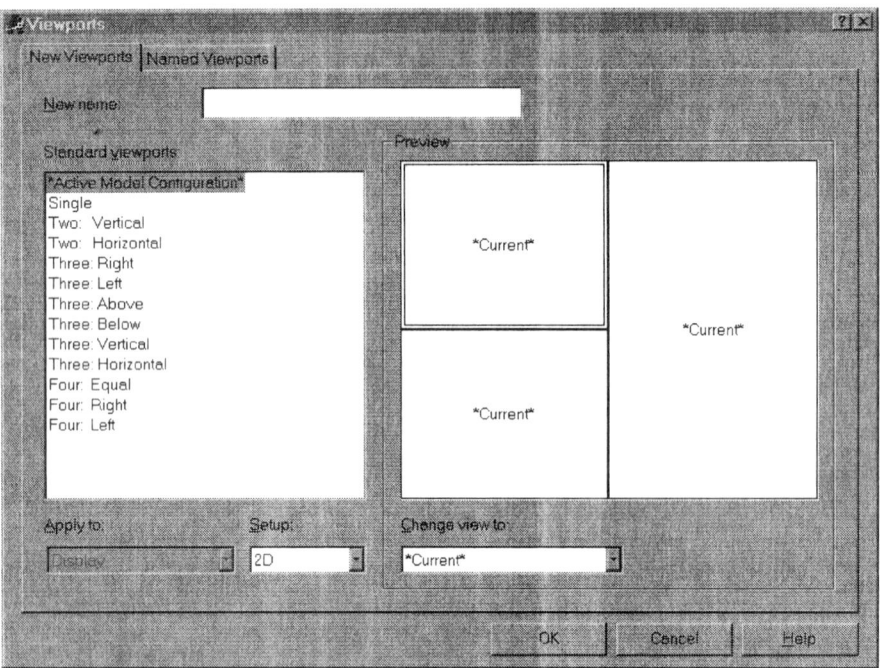

Figure 3.4 *The Viewports dialog box.*

- **1/2/3/4** - Indicates the number of viewports to be created. Once a number is selected greater than 1 the `Horizontal/<Vertical>:` prompt is displayed. Make a selection as to whether the viewports are to be created horizontally or vertically.
- **Join** - Joins two aligned viewports and creates a single viewport. The two viewports to be joined must create a single rectangular viewport.

Once the viewports are created, they must be activated before objects are created or modified within them. To activate a viewport, simply move the crosshairs to the viewport and select it. The viewport will be highlighted indicating that it is the current viewport. All commands that are available with a single viewport configuration can be used.

SKILL BUILDER

It is possible to create multiple viewports within a single viewport. While this may sound interesting, many times the viewports created are too small to be usable and AutoCAD will only allow a specific number based on the resolution of the screen.

SKILL BUILDER

Use the REGENALL command to regenerate all viewports. If this command is not used, each viewport must be activated and regenerated individually.

Section 2: Introduction to Plotting

Plotting a *scaled* drawing can be a frustrating task to accomplish in AutoCAD. This is especially true with electronic drawings because drawings are created in both US Customary and SI systems of measure.

Plotting Metric Drawings

There are basic fundamentals that must be understood before an accurate metric plot can be produced. They can be summarized with the following bullets.

- Millimeters (mm) are the basic unit of measure for electronic metric drawings.

- The conversion from inches to millimeters is 1 inch is equal to 24.5 mm.

- Selecting the MM option of the Paper Size and Orientation area of the Plot Configuration dialog box will automatically select millimeters as the plotting units. This will automatically convert all of the settings to metric.

- To plot a metric drawing at half scale, ensure that your settings are 25.4 Plotted MM = 2 Drawing Units.

Plotting Drawings with Correct Line Widths

As stated in the last unit, there are four common line widths that are used when creating technical drawings. Using Unit 2 as a reference, complete Table 3.1.

Line Width (mm)	Use(s)
	Center Lines, Dimension Lines, Leader Lines, and Boundary Lines
	Text
	Object, Connection, and Shielding
	Border

Table 3.1 *Common line widths and their uses.*

You can assign lineweights to individual layers using the Layer Properties Manager dialog box shown in figure 3.5 in much the same way you assign color and linetypes to a drawing. To assign a lineweight to a layer select Default (or the name of a currently assigned lineweight) under the Lineweight column to access the Lineweight dialog box shown in figure 3.6. You can also assign lineweights to individual objects with the Properties dialog box, which is discussed in Unit 10, Basic Editing Skills.manuals or the instructor for more information concerning these devices.

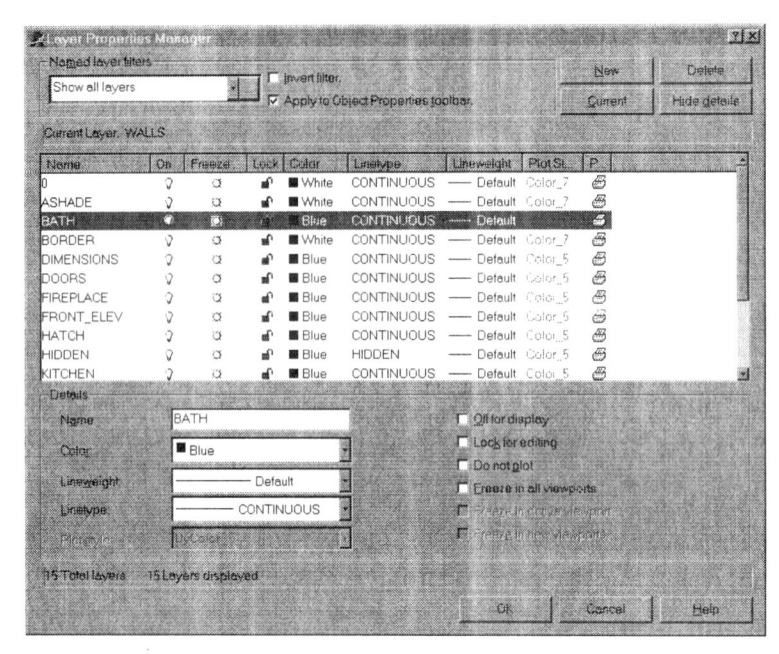

Figure 3.5 The Layer Properties Manager dialog box used to assign lineweights to individual layers.
After establishing a lineweight, everything drawn on that layer will adopt the specified lineweight. The lineweight can be toggled on and off by selecting the LWT button on the Status bar.

The procedure outlined above was meant to give a brief example of the procedures necessary to establish line thickness. A thorough explanation of layers and linetypes is given in Unit 5, Understanding Layers and Linetypes.

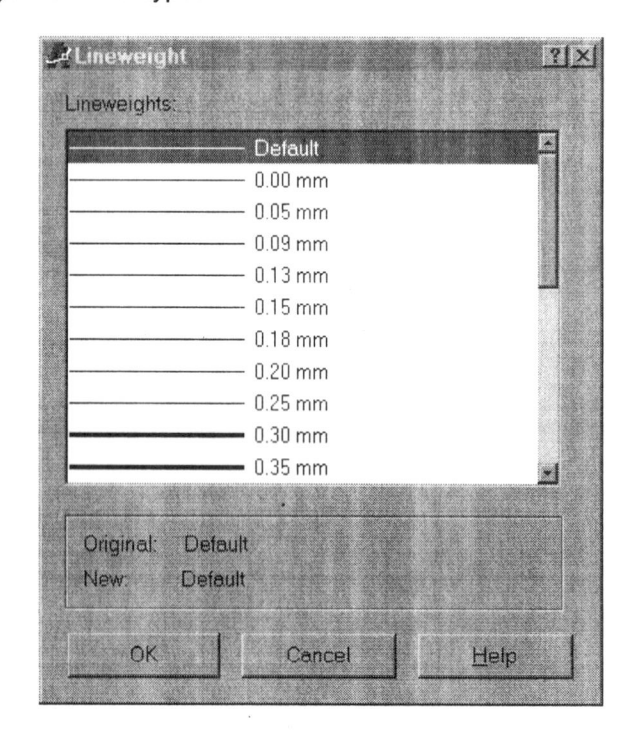

Figure 3.6 *The Lineweight dialog box.*
30

NAME _____

Unit 3 Review

1. RT stands for _Real_ _Time_.

2. The _View_ command allows views to be saved and restored.

3. The _Vports_ command allows the drawing area to be separated into one or more viewports.

4. The _Regen All_ command will perform regeneration on all viewports in a multiple viewport configuration.

5. There are _25.4_ mm in an inch.

6. Besides using the PAN and RTPAN commands, the _Aerial View or Scroll Bar_ may also be used to pan the display.

7. The _Printer Plot_ command will create a hardcopy of an AutoCAD drawing.

8. True or **False**. The only way to add thickness to lines on hardcopy is to assign a lineweight to them.

9. **True** or False. Previously saved views may be selected and plotted.

10. **True** or False. The configuration for one hardcopy device can be used for all hardcopy devices.

Unit 3 Assignment #1

In this assignment you plot the *Angle Block* drawing that you created in the previous unit. Follow the steps below to assist you in plotting these drawings.

1. Load the *Angle Block* file.

2. Execute the PLOT command.

3. Plot the drawing using limits or extents.

4. Plot at a scale of 1 Plotted Inch equal to 1 Drawing Unit.

Unit 3 Assignment #2

In this assignment you will plot the *Block Diagram* drawing that you created in the previous unit. Follow the steps below to assist you in plotting this drawing.

1. Load the *Block Diagram* file.

2. Execute the PLOT command.

3. Plot the drawing using limits or extents.

4. Plot at a scale of 1 Plotted Inch equal to 1 Drawing Unit.

Unit 4: Basic CAD Drawing Techniques

Overview

Most mechanical drawings use the decimal form of units. You will first learn how to set decimal units and precision of units commonly used in mechanical CAD drawings. Next you will set up a prototype drawing. This prototype drawing will be used in later units to speed up and standardize the drawing process.

Objectives

- Set the decimal display format and precision.
- Create a prototype drawing for English and metric.
- Begin a new drawing by using the prototype drawings.
- Create geometry for an electronic drawing using the coordinate system of data entry.

Introduction

Most electronic drawings use a decimal type of scale, such as 4.25". Even though you will set your units to decimal for electronic drawings, AutoCAD allows you to use any type of units in your drawing. If it is more convenient to enter information in feet and inches, for example, you can change your units at any time. Changing units or entering units in a different format will not affect any other objects in the drawing.

A drawing template normally contains values for limits, grid, and snap. After setting the correct units, you will create a drawing template containing the values for limits, grid, and snap commonly used in electronic drawings. Drawing templates will be created for metric as well as English drawings.

Section 1: Setting Display Format and Precision (UNITS and DDUNITS)

To set the units, access the Drawing Units dialog box. This can be accomplished by doing the following:

- Choose Units from Data on the menu bar.
- Enter **units** at the Command: prompt.

Although AutoCAD has five different measurement report formats, decimal units are generally used in electronic drafting, because ANSI Y14.5M Dimensioning and Tolerancing standards specify that decimal inch units or metric units in millimeters be used in engineering drawings. AutoCAD can display a maximum of eight decimal places. Decimal is the default type of unit in AutoCAD.

After setting the measurement report format to decimal units, the next step is to set the display precision. AutoCAD rounds the value of the display, so two digits may be shown as 2.88, three digits as 2.875, and four digits as 2.8751. Regardless of what you set the display precision at, AutoCAD is accurate to 14 decimal places.

For electronic drawings, three to four digit display precision is normally used for inch drawings. For metric drawings, one or two-place decimals are generally used, such as 16.5 or 16.50. This difference is due to the greater distance represented by inches as opposed to millimeters.

Angular Measurement

Angular measurement is also set in the Drawing Units dialog box. AutoCAD has five different angular measurement options. Decimal degrees are generally used in electrical drafting, which is the default type of angular measurement in AutoCAD.

Decimal degrees display angular measurement as real numbers with up to eight decimal places, such as 42.500. Two place decimal degrees are normally used for electrical drawings.

Tutorial 4.1: Setting Units and Angular Measurement

In this tutorial you will set the units and angular measurement for a metric drawing.

1. From the Standard toolbar, select New. If prompted with the Save Changes dialog box, select No. In the Create New Drawing dialog box, enter the proper path, name the drawing MDEFAULT, then select OK.

2. Choose Data/Units.

3. Set the units to Decimal with zero digits for Precision.

4. Set the angles to Decimal Degrees, precision 0 (AutoCAD default). Your Drawing Units dialog box should look like figure 4.1.

5. Choose OK to close the Drawing Units dialog box. The next tutorial will continue from here.

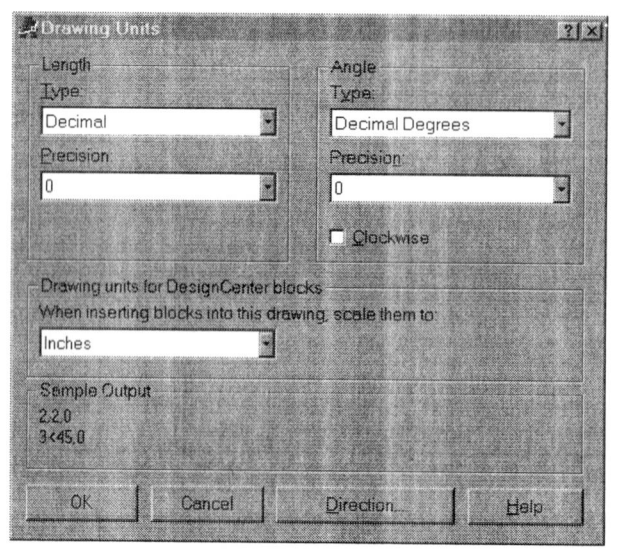

Figure 4.1 *The units and angular measurement for a metric drawing.*

Section 2: Working with Drawing Templates

A drawing template is a file that will be used when a new drawing is created. Proper use of a template drawing can save work. When you begin a new drawing you normally set different variables, such as the limits, snap increment, and grid spacing. The advantage of using a template drawing is that it frees you from having to change these same settings every time you start a new drawing.

Tutorial 4.2: Creating a Metric Drawing Template

In this tutorial you will create a metric drawing template. You will set the limits, grid, and snap to values commonly used in a metric A-size drawing.

1. Continue from the previous tutorial.

2. Choose Format/Drawing Limits.

3. At the `Specify lower left corner or [ON/OFF] <0,0>:` prompt, press Enter.

4. At the `Specify upper right corner <12,9>:` prompt, type **230,170** and press Enter. To show the entire limits within the view window, issue a ZOOM ALL option:

5. From the Standard toolbar, choose the Zoom All icon. After the limits are established, you will set the grid to 4 and the snap to 2.

6. Choose Tools/Drafting Settings to access the Drafting Settings dialog box.

7. Make sure the Snap and Grid tab is selected and enter **4** for the grid X and Y spacing.

8. Enter **2** for the snap X and Y spacing.

9. Check the Snap On and Grid On check boxes. Your dialog box should appear as shown in figure 4.2.

10. The MDEFAULT template is now ready to be saved. To save the template, select Save As... from the File pulldown menu. Once the Save Drawing As dialog box is displayed, select Drawing Template File from the Save as type drop-down menu. Select the proper path to save the template file and then select Save.

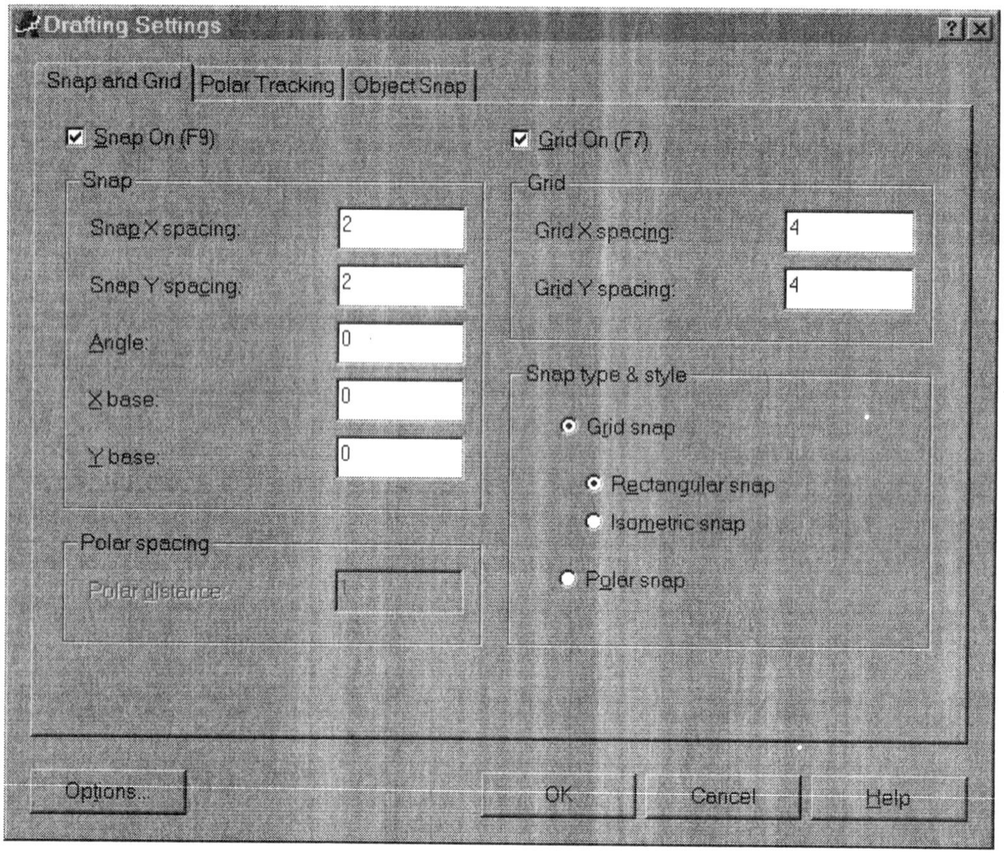

Figure 4.2 *Setting the grid to 4 and the snap to 2 for a metric drawing.*

Section 3: Coordinate System Basics

Even though you may have set grid and snap modes in your prototype drawing, any coordinate entered through the keyboard overrides these settings. This is true even if the desired point location does not fall on the grid or cannot be snapped to, or if the To point: location is at an angle to the previous location with ortho mode turned on.

Remember, you can switch the coordinate entry method at any time during a command sequence. The first coordinate may be absolute, followed by a relative move, an absolute polar coordinate, and then using the pointing device. You can also change the type of units at any time during the drawing. For example, even though your units are set to decimal, you can enter values in feet and inches if it is more convenient. Changing the coordinate entry method will not affect any other objects previously created in your drawing.

NAME _____

Unit 4 Review

1. The type of units normally used for mechanical English drawings is _____ with a display precision of _____ digits.

2. The type of units normally used for mechanical metric drawings is _____ with a display precision of _____ digits.

3. The _____ standard specifies drawing parameters for use in mechanical drafting.

4. Angular measurement should be set to _____ for English mechanical drawings with _____ decimal places.

5. The suggested drawing area for a standard A-size English drawing is _____ x _____.

6. To draw a line 6 units long at 45 degrees from the current point using polar coordinates, you would enter _____ at the To point: prompt.

7. Regardless of what units or display precision are used, AutoCAD is accurate to _____ decimal places.

8. The measurements for a B-size sheet of paper are _____ x _____ inches.

9. To convert inches to millimeters, multiply the inch value by _____.

10. Two variables commonly set in a prototype drawing are _____ and _____.

39

Unit 4 Assignment #1

1. Create an electrical English template drawing using the following settings:

    Units = Decimal

    Precision = 2

    Limits = 9 x 7

    Snap = .125

    Grid = .250

2. Save the drawing as a template named *Edefault.dwt*.

Unit 4 Assignment #2

1. Begin a new drawing, naming it 02DWG01.

2. Open the Polar Tracking settings. Set the Increment angle to 45 degrees. Make sure Polar Tracking On is checked.

3. While still in the Drafting Settings dialog box, switch to the Snap and Grid tab. Pick Polar Snap as the snap type, and set the Polar distance to 1. make sure Snap is on, and pick OK to close the dialog box.

4. Use the LINE command to draw figure 4.3, starting with the lower left corner at the point 2,2. All angles are increments of 45 degrees. Use the snap setting to get the correct distances.

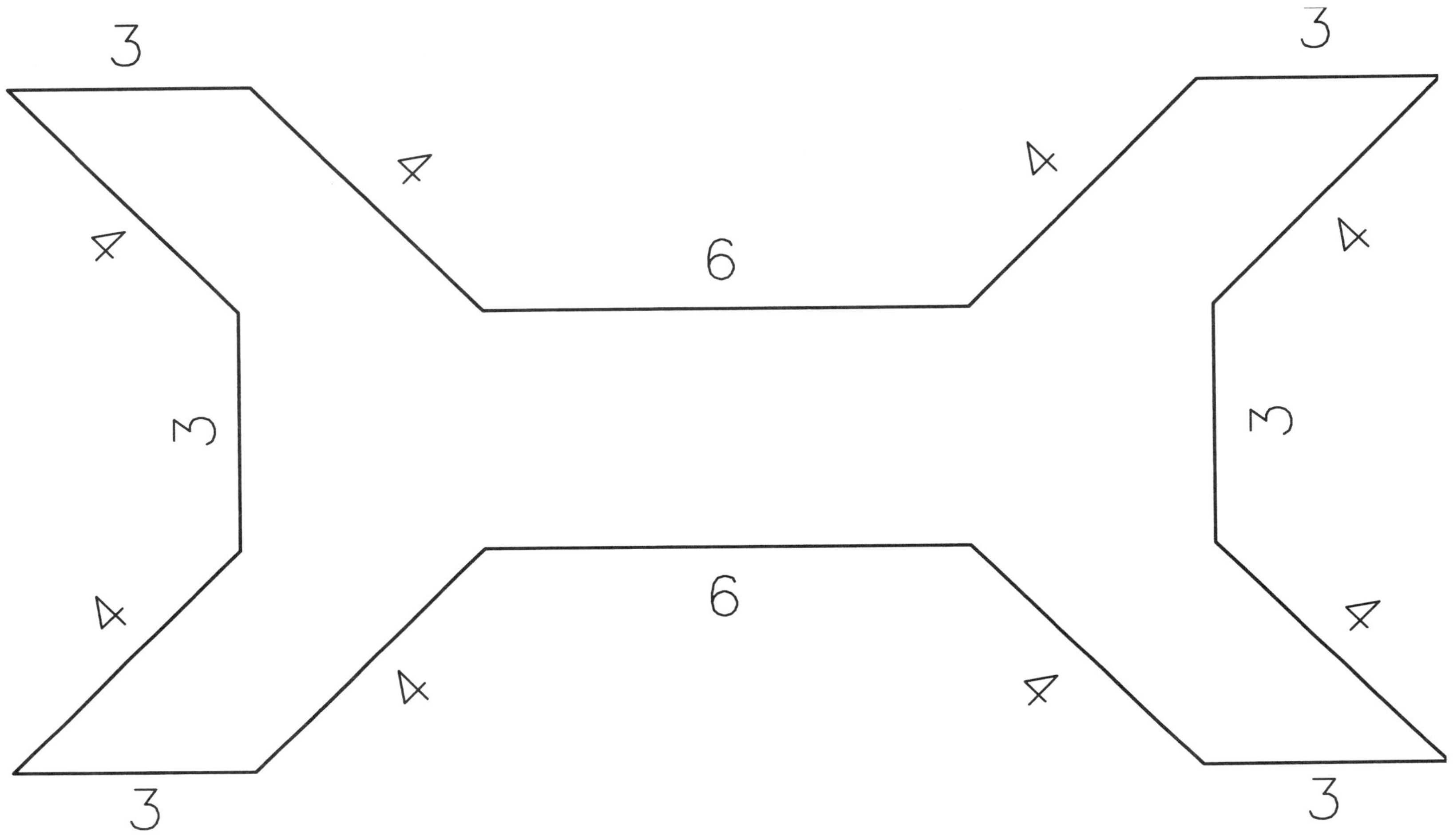

Figure 4.3 *Draw the figure using Polar Tracking and Polar Snap.*

Unit 5: Understanding Layers and Linetypes

Overview

Correct use of layers and linetypes is a fundamental aspect of any electronic CAD drawing. The International Organization for Standardization (ISO) has developed a standard for organization and naming of layers for CAD. The American National Standards Institute (ANSI) is in the process of adopting the standards of organization and naming of layers for CAD proposed by the International Organization for Standardization (ISO) for electronic drawings. In this unit you will learn about the ISO layer naming standard, and also the ANSI linetype standard. You will then apply these principles to the prototype drawings that you created in the previous unit.

Objectives

- Create layers for electronic components.
- Assign linetypes to layers.
- Create a Metric drawing template for use in a schematic drawing.

Introduction

In electrical CAD drawings, proper use of layers is essential. In many projects several different drafters may work on the same drawing. One drafter may be responsible for component placement. Another may be responsible for wiring. Often geometry created in one drawing may be used in another. The printed circuit board assembly may be used to create an artwork view. Proper naming of layers is essential in all CAD drawings to ensure standardization in a company.

Along with layers, there are also standards available for linetypes. AutoCAD contains a predefined alphabet of lines, including several that conform to ISO standard linetypes.

Section 1: Working with Layers

Standardizing layer names and content is an extremely important aspect of CAD drawing. In a typical electrical drawing, you may easily have over 100 layers. In a schematic drawing for example, you may have separate layers for resistors, capacitors, diodes, and switches.

Without standardization, it becomes virtually impossible to have different people work on a project. In many cases you may be required to work on a drawing that was originally started by someone else. Imagine trying to determine which layer contains the wiring from a list containing over 100 layer names!

Naming Layers

The structure of an electrical drawing is normally defined in the standards of a firm. Layer names should coincide with the type of component that will reside on the layer. Table 5.1 lists several components commonly found in a typical schematic and layer names.

Component Name	Layer Name
Operational Amplifier	OPAMP
Normal Capacitor	CAP
Multicell Battery	MBAT
Ground, Earth/Power Line	GND1
Ground, Chassis	GND2
Wiring	WIRE
Dashed Line	DASHLINE

Table 5.1 *Component and layer naming.*

Adding New Layers

You can add layers at any time with the Layer Control dialog box, which is accessed by entering `ddlmodes` at the `Command:` prompt, or by selecting the Layers button on the Object Properties toolbar.

Tutorial 5.1: Creating a Drawing Template with Layers

For this tutorial, you will begin a new drawing and create layers for use in a metric drawing. You will follow the ISO layer naming conventions.

1. Select the Open button from the Standard toolbar and load the MDEFAULT template drawing you created in Unit 4.

2. Choose the Layers button from the Object Properties toolbar.

3. The Layer Control dialog box appears.

4. Choose New and enter OPAMP. This layer is now added to the Layer Control dialog box.

5. Continue creating the layers shown in Table 5.1.

6. Don't close the drawing or dialog box; the next tutorial continues from here.

Changing the Layer Color

When a specific color is assigned to a layer, all objects drawn on that layer will display the assigned color. By assigning colors to different objects on the drawing, the drawing is much easier to read. If all dimensions are blue, for example, it becomes much easier to see the part boundary. If you are plotting to an output device that has color capabilities, you can also take advantage of the colors assigned to the layers and plot the drawing in color.

To change the colors of a specific layer, select the layer in the Layer Control dialog box. The layer name becomes highlighted, and you can select the Set Color box on the right. Notice that you can also select more than one layer at a time if you want to assign the same color to several different layers.

Tutorial 5.2: Changing Layer Color

In this tutorial you will change layer colors for the layers you created in the previous tutorial.

1. Select the Layers button from the standard toolbar. Select the OPAMP layer.

2. This layer becomes highlighted, and you can now select the Set Color box on the right.

3. Choose the Color button.

4. Choose the standard color Green. Notice that the word "green" appears in the Color edit box.

5. Continue changing the colors of the following layers:

Layer Name	Color
CAP	64
MBAT	13
GND1	145
GND2	155
WIRE	RED
DASHLINE	YELLOW

6. Select OK to close the dialog box; the next tutorial continues from here.

Section 2: Understanding Linetypes

Another important aspect of electronic drawings is the use of linetypes. The line conventions endorsed by the American National Standards Institute, ANSI Y14.2-M-1979 (R1987), are commonly used in many electrical drawings. This section discusses the use of American National Standards Institute (ANSI) linetypes and how to apply them to your layers.

While AutoCAD has a wide variety of linetypes already created, including linetypes meeting the ISO (International Organization of Standards) standard, ANSI linetypes are not apparently available. You must be sure to select the ISO standard linetype that most closely matches the required ANSI linetype. ISO linetypes are based on the ANSI standards.

What Are Linetypes?

A linetype is simply a repeating pattern of dots, dashes, and blank spaces. In manual drafting drawing a linetype can be a very tedious process, where you constantly measure and draw short dashes and spaces. Drawing with a CAD system makes this process much easier. When a linetype is defined in AutoCAD, the linetype name and its corresponding definition determine the specific sequence and relative lengths of dashes, dots, and blank spaces. When you use the linetype to create an object, AutoCAD automatically re-creates the specific sequence of dashes, dots, and blank spaces.

Most electronic drawings contain a variety of different linetypes. A certain type of line may be used on a drawing to represent a hidden surface. Other lines may be used to represent the center point of circles or arcs.

Loading and Setting the Linetype

A linetype must be loaded before it can be assigned to a layer. This can be done in the Layer dialog box. To assign a linetype to a layer, select the applicable layers and choose the Linetype option. By default, the standard AutoCAD linetypes are located in the acad.lin file located in the c:/Program Files/AutoCAD R14/Support: subdirectory. Other linetype files can be created to this file. Linetypes are assigned to a given layer so that all objects drawn on that layer will have those linetypes automatically.

Tutorial 5.3: Loading and Setting ISO Linetypes

In this tutorial you will load and set linetypes for the layers you created in the previous tutorial.

1. Select the Layers button from the standard toolbar. The Layer Properties Manager dialog box will be displayed.

2. Select the DASHLINE layer.

   This layer becomes highlighted,

3. Select the Linetype option next to the layer name. The Select Linetype dialog box is displayed.

4. Select the Load... button. The Load or Reload dialog box is displayed.

5. Select the ISODASH linetype.

6. Select the OK button to close the Load or Reload dialog box.

7. Select the OK button to close the Layer dialog box.

8. Save the file.

Understanding Linetype Scale (LTSCALE)

Linetypes are defined by a series of dashes and spaces. The LTSCALE command is used to change the relative scale of the dashes and spaces that define a linetype. As long as the LTSCALE is set to 1.0 (the default), the length of the dashes and spaces you defined for the linetypes will remain the same.

Most electronics drawings are created full-size. When the drawing is plotted, it remains full-size while the plot is scaled. If the drawing is going to be plotted at full scale (1=1), the default linetype scale is fine. If the drawing is going to be plotted at a different scale, you need to change the size of the linetype by increasing the value of the linetype scale (to 4, for example, if the plot scale is 1=4).

You may have noticed in the previous tutorials that we were working on a Metric drawing template, but defined the size of the ANSI linetypes in inches. By changing the LTSCALE of the metric prototype drawing, the size of the ANSI linetypes is adjusted accordingly. In this example, the LTSCALE should be set to 25.4, since 1 inch = 25.4 millimeters. You can change the linetype scale by using the following method:

- Enter **ltscale** at the Command: prompt.

This will set the linetype scale for all linetypes in the entire drawing. After you set a new linetype scale factor, AutoCAD automatically regenerates the drawing unless you have the automatic regen turned off.

Name _____

Unit 5 Review

1. The two organizations offering standards for linetypes are _____ and _____.

2. ANSI stands for _____ _____ _____ _____.

3. ISO stands for _____ _____ _____.

4. A linetype is defined as a series of _____ and _____.

5. To distinguish different components and wiring on an electrical drawing, proper use of _____, _____, and _____ is essential.

6. To filter layer names, the symbol for a wild card is _____.

7. The following linetype pattern, A,0.625,-.125 will create a space of _____.

8. In question 7, changing the LTSCALE to 2 for the linetype pattern will create a space of _____.

9. The value used to change inches to millimeters is _____.

10. By default, AutoCAD contains linetypes meeting the _____ standard.

Unit 5 Assignment #1

In this assignment you will create various schematic symbols, using the MDEFAULT drawing template.

1. Create a new drawing using the MDEFAULT drawing template with layers and linetypes that was created in this unit.

2. Draw the symbols shown in figure 5.1 on the correct layer.

3. Save the drawing as SCHEMATIC.

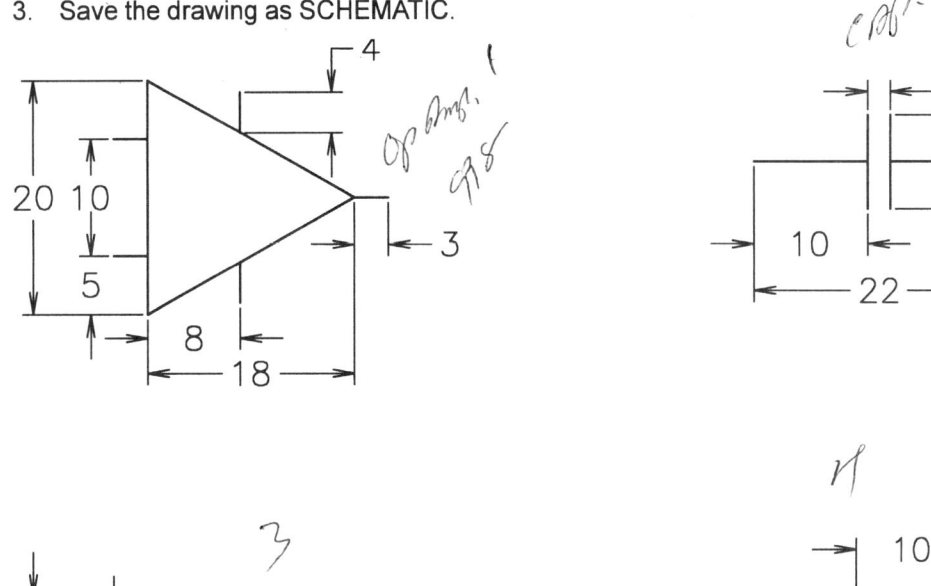

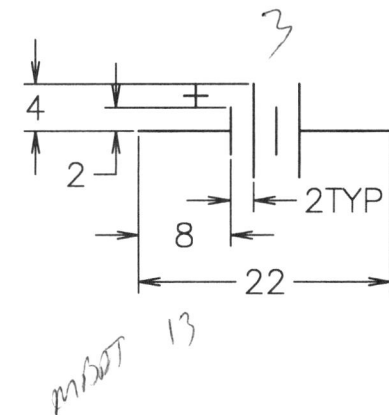

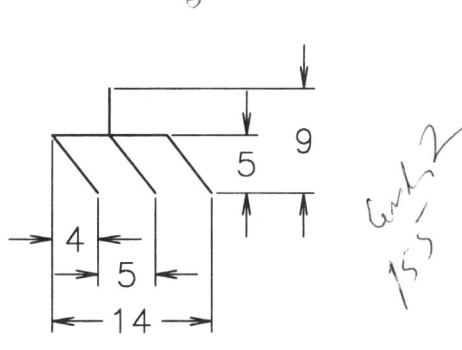

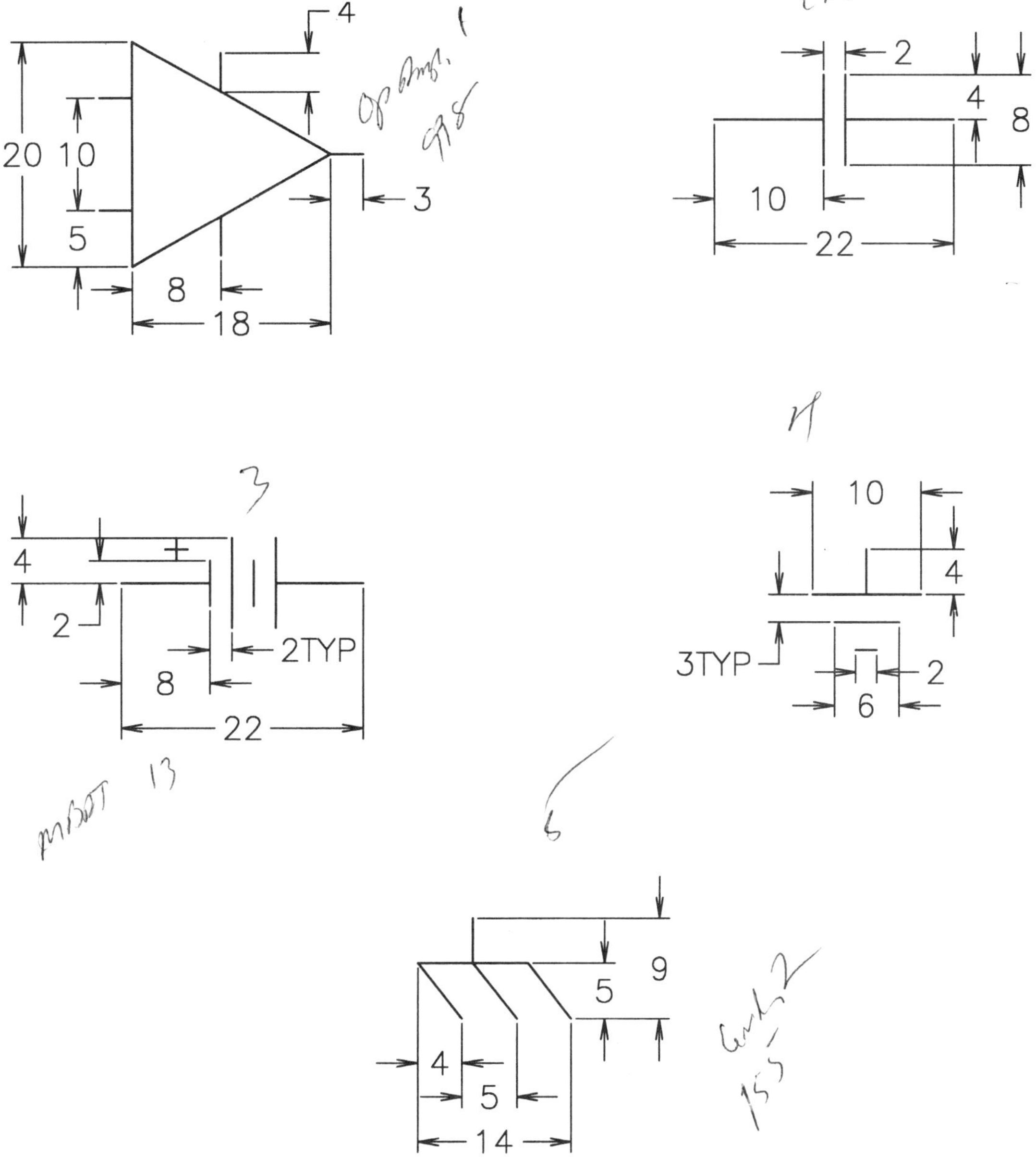

Figure 5.1 *The electrical symbols.*

53

Unit 5 Assignment #2

In this assignment you will create various schematic symbols, using the MDEFAULT drawing template.

1. Create a new drawing using the MDEFAULT drawing template with layers and linetypes that was created in this unit.

2. Create a new layer, CAPC01 color 64.

3. Draw the symbol for a .01 uF capacitor shown in figure 5.2.

4. Save the drawing as PCB.

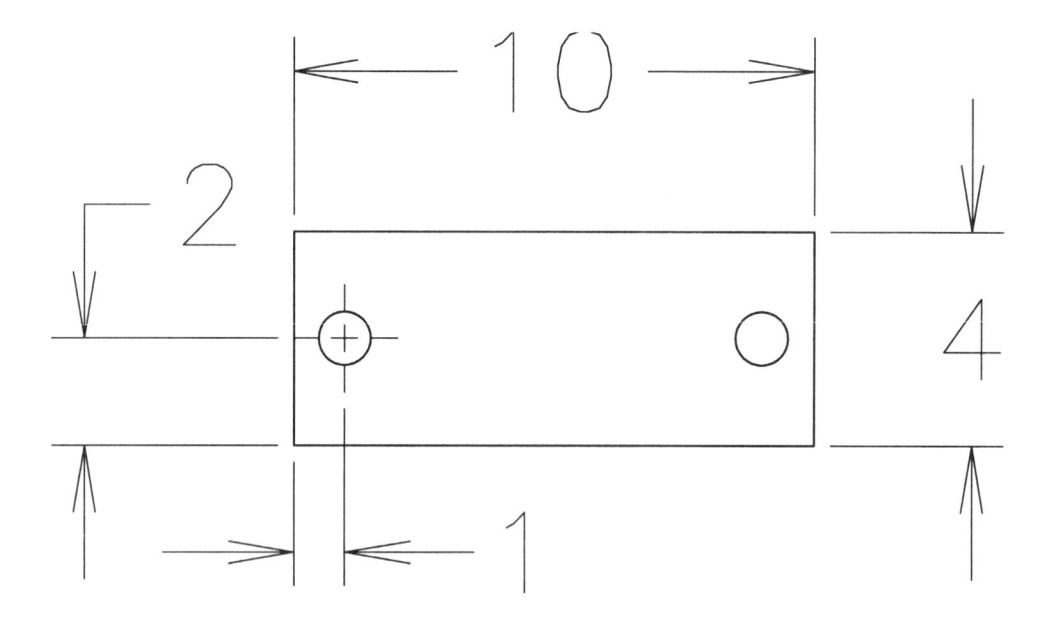

Figure 5.2 *The capacitor symbol drawing for use in a printed circuit board.*

Unit 6: Creating Basic Geometry

Overview

Most electrical symbols, schematics, and printed circuit boards consist of basic geometry. Circles, lines, and arcs make up the majority of geometry in a typical electrical drawing. In this unit you will use these commands and the skills developed previously to create basic electronic symbols that will contribute to the development of an existing schematic drawing.

Objectives

- Draw circles with the CIRCLE command.
- Draw arcs with two common ARC commands.

Introduction

In this unit you will apply some of the basic AutoCAD commands to create a fuse symbol shown in figure 6.1. To do this, you will apply the CIRCLE and ARC commands.

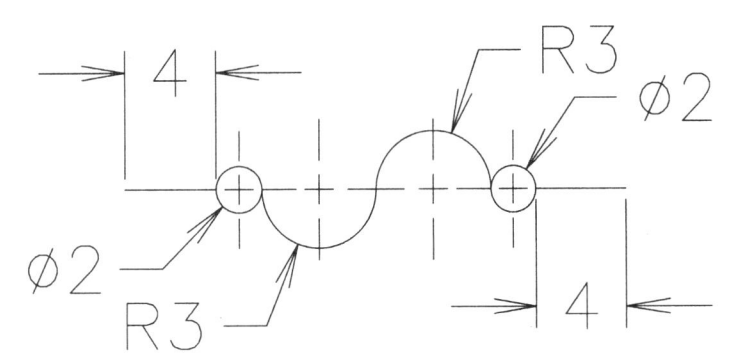

Figure 6.1 *The CIRCLE and ARC commands are used to create the fuse symbol.*

Drawing Circles (CIRCLE)

The CIRCLE command is commonly used to represent contact points on electrical drawings. A circle is also used in a variety of electrical symbols, including those for lamps and light emitting diodes.

Tutorial 6.1: Beginning the Fuse Symbol

In this tutorial you will open the SCHEMATIC drawing you created in Unit 5, and create the circle used in the fuse symbol.

Begin by choosing Open from the standard toolbar. Change to the proper drive and directory and open the SCHEMATIC drawing.

1. Select the Layer button from the Object Properties toolbar. Create a new layer using the following parameters and set it as the current layer:

2. Make sure the Draw floating toolbar appears on your screen. Select the Circle button from the Draw toolbar.

3. Enter the absolute coordinates for the center point for the circle and the diameter.

   ```
   [3P/2P/Ttr (tan tan radius)]: 100,150
   ```

   ```
   Specify radius of circle or [Diameter]: 1
   ```

   Select the Line button from the Draw toolbar and enter the following points:

   ```
   Specify first point: 95,150
   ```

   ```
   Specify next point or [Undo]: 99,150
   ```

   ```
   Specify next point or [Undo]:
   ```

4. Press the Zoom Window button on the standard toolbar and zoom in on the fuse symbol.

5. Press the Save button to save your drawing. The next tutorial will continue from here. Your drawing should look like figure 6.2

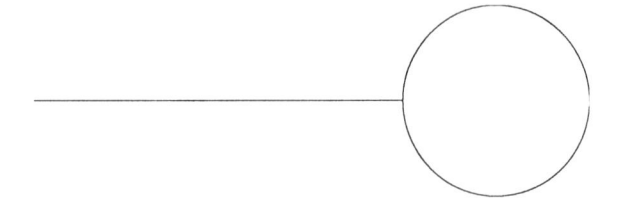

Figure 6.2 *Creating the left line and a circle for the fuse symbol.*

Drawing Arcs (ARC)

In addition to circles, many electrical parts contain rounded sections and arcs. While AutoCAD contains 11 different methods for drawing an arc, the most common are the three point, start-center-end, and start-end-radius methods. While the 11 different options can seem overwhelming, all of the methods are based on the starting point, starting direction, center point, included angle, endpoint, lengths of chord, and radius of an arc.

Before deciding which arc command to use, evaluate the arc you need to draw. Determine what you know about the arc, and match up the known information to one of the different options. The different icons available for ARC appear on the fly-out menu. The information needed to create the particular arc appears at the bottom of the AutoCAD display. For example, when you hold the pointing device over the Arc Start Center End button, it says "Creates an arc using the start point, center and end point" at the bottom of the AutoCAD display.

Tutorial 6.2: Creating Arcs with 3 Point and Arc Continue

Using two common methods of drawing an arc, you will put the rounded portion on the symbol.

1. Continue from the previous tutorial.

2. Select Draw/Arc/3 Points pull-down menu.

   `Specify start point of arc or [CEnter]: 101,150`

   `Specify second point of arc or [CEnter/ENd]: 104,153`

   `Specify end point of arc: 107,150`

3. Select the Draw/Arc/Continue pull-down menu.

4. Notice that the next arc begins at the end of the previous arc. The only information you need to supply is the end point.

   `Specify end point of arc: @6<0`

   Your drawing should now look similar to figure 6.3.

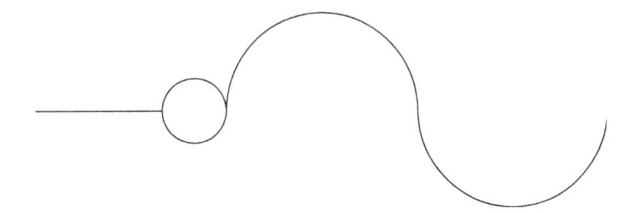

Figure 6.3 *Drawing arcs with 3 Point and Start, End, Radius.*

5. Complete the symbol by adding the circle and line on the end of the second arc as shown in figure 6.1.

6. Select the Save button on the standard toolbar to save the fuse symbol on the SCHEMATIC drawing.

57

NAME _____

Unit 6 Review

1. Arcs and circles are drawn in a _____ direction.

2. An arc may be drawn through _____ degrees.

3. When using the 3 point arc command, you can mark the second point of an arc by using _____, _____, or _____ coordinates.

4. AutoCAD contains _____ different methods for drawing an arc.

5. All of the methods for drawing an arc are based on one or a combination of the following information: _____, _____, _____, _____, _____, _____, and _____.

6. When defining a POLYGON, the maximum number of sides it can contain is _____.

7. When you create a rectangle, it is drawn as a _____.

8. To edit the individual segments of an object created with the RECTANGLE command, use the _____ command.

9. The system variable that stores the diameter or radius of the most recently created circle is _____.

10. An inscribed polygon is contained _____ an imaginary circle on which the polygon is based.

Unit 6 Assignment #1

In this assignment you will add newly created electronic symbols to a previously created schematic drawing.

1. Open the SCHEMATIC drawing you created previously and create the different electronic symbols as shown in figure 6.4.

2. Create the following layers:

Layer	Component Name	Color	Linetype
LXIFMR	Iron Core Transformer	87	Continuous
ECAP	Electrolytic Capacitor	30	Continuous
PLUG	Plug	85	Continuous
RES	Resistor	171	Continuous

3. Save the schematic drawing with the new symbols.

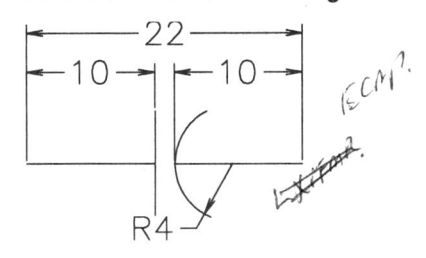

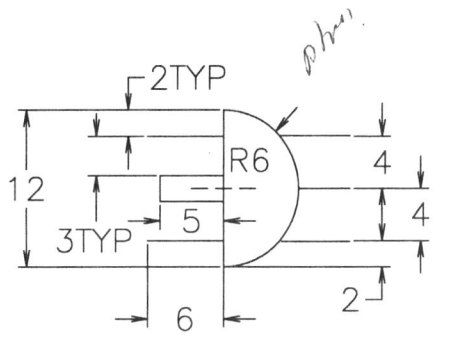

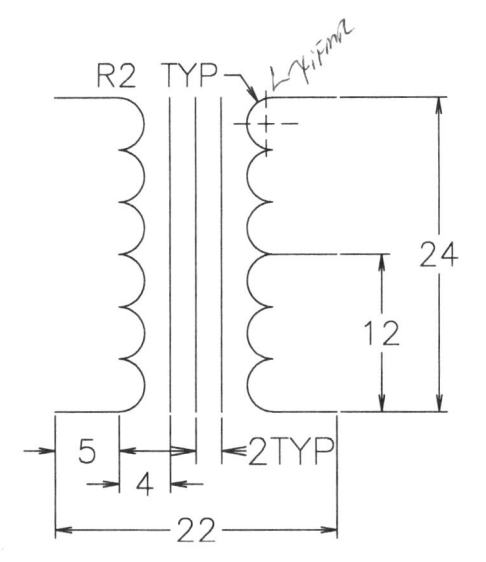

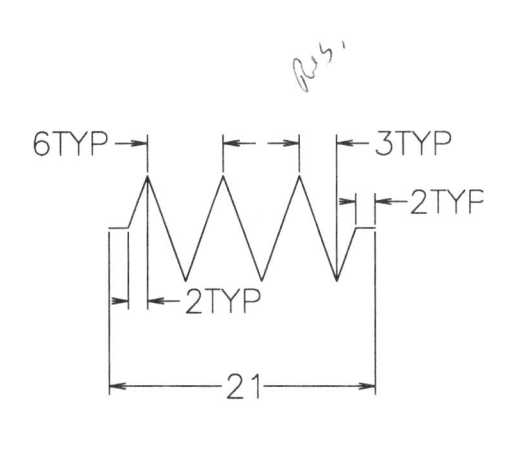

Figure 6.4 *Create the electrical symbols in the SCHEMATIC drawing.*

Unit 6 Assignment #2

In this assignment you will add newly created electronic symbols to a previously created schematic drawing.

1. Open the SCHEMATIC drawing you created previously and create the inductor and transistor symbols as shown in figure 6.5.

2. Create the following layers:

Layer	Component Name	Color	Linetype
PTRAN	PNP Transistor	132	Continuous
INDUC	Inductor	55	Continuous

3. Save the SCHEMATIC drawing with the new symbols.

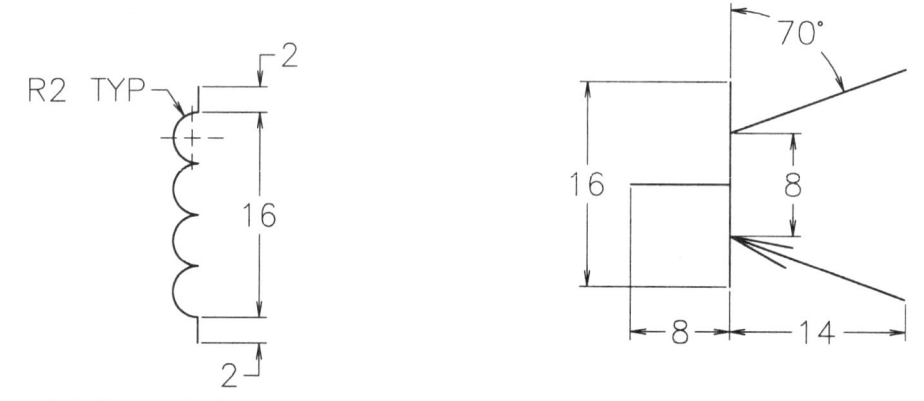

Figure 6.5 *Create the inductor and transistor symbols.*

1. Create a new drawing called COLLECTOR, using the SCHEMATIC drawing as a template.

2. Use the symbols you created in the SCHEMATIC drawing to draw the common collector, shown in figure 6.6.

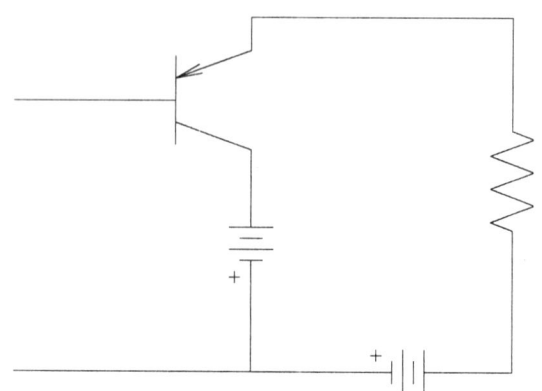

Figure 6.6 *Draw the common collector.*

Unit 7: Annotating a Drawing with Text and Hatching

Overview

Almost every drawing you create will contain some type of text. At the very least, the name of the person creating the drawing is included. Text is also commonly used to create notes and a parts list. Many electrical drawings also make use of hatching to depict the outside border of a printed circuit board.

Objectives

- Use text styles (STYLE) for electrical drawings.
- Select a font for electrical drawings.
- Name the text style.
- Set the text height for electrical drawings.
- Enter text and change the style.
- Use ANSI and ISO hatch patterns.

Introduction

The LINE, CIRCLE, ARC and POLYGON commands can be used to make the majority of the geometry required in electrical drawings. Most drawings contain more than just geometry, however. Almost every drawing you create will contain some type of text, such as in dimensioning and notes. Adding text in manual drafting can be a long and tedious process. Using a CAD system greatly simplifies this process. Properly applied, all text on a CAD drawing will be perfect.

In addition to text, many electrical drawings contain some type of hatching. Hatching is often used on the border of a printed circuit board assembly view to show the location of the outside border.

Section 1: Adding Text to a Drawing

AutoCAD allows you to use a wide variety of fonts in your drawing. Fonts provided with AutoCAD have the (.SHX) extension. In addition to the .SHX fonts, you can also use True Type fonts (.TTF). Many programs provide their own fonts, and as long as they have one of the file extensions listed above, they can be used in a drawing. With the ability to use a wide variety of different font types in a drawing, your possibilities are almost limitless!

Selecting the Correct Font

The design of modern alphabets originated in Egyptian hieroglyphics. Over time, these hieroglyphics evolved into a cursive hieratic style of writing. Originally, the Roman capital alphabet consisted of 22 different characters. These characters have remained practically unchanged to this day. The wide variety of font styles we see today were derived from the design of the original Roman capitals. With the wide variety of font styles available, not to mention variations on a style (such as boldface or italic), selecting the proper font can be hard.

As industry and technical drawing in the United States developed, a need for simple, legible letters that could be executed with single strokes of an ordinary pen arose. From this need the American National Standards Institute [ANSI Y14.2M-1979 (R1987)] standard evolved. The lettering forms suggested by ANSI apply to CAD as well as manual drafting.

Lettering on a CAD drawing must be legible and suitable for easy and quick output. Complex fonts can significantly slow down regeneration times, as well as plotting. Either vertical or inclined letters may be used, but only *one style* should appear on any drawing. It is also not desirable to vary the size of the letters in a drawing. The font style recommended that meets the ANSI standard is the Roman Simplex style. This style is included with AutoCAD.

Defining a Text Style for Electrical Drawings (STYLE)

As mentioned previously, the font style that meets the ANSI standard is the Roman Simplex font, included with AutoCAD. Its filename is ROMANS.SHX and it is located in the Program Files/AutoCAD R14/fonts subdirectory. The best way to define the different text styles is with the Text Style dialog box shown in figure 7.1. You can access the Text Style dialog box as follows:

- Select Text Style from the Format pull down menu.
- Type **style** at the Command: prompt.

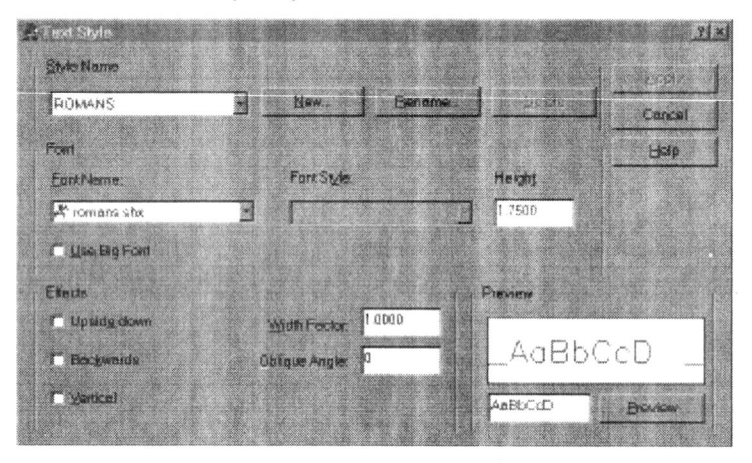

Figure 7.1 *The Text Style dialog box is used to define the different text styles used in a drawing.*

The procedure for creating a text style is as follows:

1. **Name the Style.** Give your new style a name. For ease in naming the style, include the name of the font used (ROMANS) with its size.

2. **Select a Font.** After naming your new style, select the ROMANS.SHX font. In electrical drawings, uniformity of the text is essential. The ROMANS.SHX font should be the foundation for all text within the drawing.

3. **Preview the Font.** The Character Preview window will provide a graphical picture of the ROMANS.SHX font.

4. **Set the Height Factor.** To ensure uniformity, set a default height for each text style.

Naming the Text Style

Following the guidelines given in the ANSI standard for font style and size, name the font based on the style selected and the size of the font. For example, you are now using the ROMANS.SHX font. If the height of the style is 2, name the style ROMANS2.

Selecting the Roman Simplex Font

To select the Roman Simplex Font select the down arrow in the Font Name window. Scroll down until you see "romans.shx."

Setting the Text Height

Because uniformity is essential in electrical drawings, setting a default value for the height will ensure standardization throughout your drawing. By entering a text height, a constant value is applied to the style when it is used in the DTEXT, MTEXT, or TEXT commands. The remaining effects, such as width factor and obliquing angle, should be left at their default setting.

Entering Text and Changing the Style

After defining the text styles, you can enter text into your drawing using the TEXT or DTEXT commands. Any text you enter will use the style that is current.

You can change the current text style by:

- **Text Style dialog box**. Access the Text Style dialog box and select the new style you want current. Select Apply, Close.
- **Type Style or (s) at the initial prompt**. At the [Justify/Style]: prompt, enter s. Type in the name of the new style, or type a ? to list styles that are currently available.

Section 2: Filling Areas with Hatching

Hatching is often used in electrical drawings to display the noncomponent area (outside perimeter) of a printed circuit board. Often the hatch pattern selected is used to indicate the material used to produce the noncomponent area of the board. The pattern may represent a specific material. AutoCAD contains a wide variety of hatch patterns that conform to the ANSI and ISO standards.

Defining the Pattern Type

AutoCAD contains a number of predefined hatch patterns meeting the ISO and ANSI standards. These patterns are stored in the ACAD.PAT file. If you select an ISO hatch pattern, you can also set the ISO pen width. If you select an ISO pen width from the pop-down list, AutoCAD automatically sets the pattern scaling in relation to the ISO linetype.

Name _____

Unit 7 Review

1. Fonts supplied with AutoCAD have the _____ file extension.

2. In addition to the fonts supplied by AutoCAD, you can also use _____ fonts.

3. The _____ _____ _____ _____ lists standards that should be applied to lettering style and height for electrical drawings.

4. The _____ _____ font is supplied by AutoCAD and meets the ANSI standard, and it should be used in electrical drawings.

5. The _____ command will allow you to display and plot text as a box.

6. Hatch patterns created with bhatch are _____, meaning the hatch is automatically updated when the boundary changes.

7. You can edit text with the _____, _____, and _____ commands.

8. AutoCAD contains predefined hatch patterns that meet the _____ and _____ standards.

9. The hatch pattern used on the exposed interior of a section part is often used to indicate _____ .

10. The predefined hatch patterns supplied with AutoCAD are stored in the _____ file.

Unit 7 Assignment #1

Open the PCB drawing you created in Unit 5 and create the following text styles. Use the ROMANS.SHX font file for all styles.

Style Name	Size	Use
ROMANS2	2	Notes and tables
ROMANS3	3	Table headings

Unit 7 Assignment #2

1. Open the PCB drawing you worked on in the previous assignment.

2. Create the parts list for use in a printed circuit board drawing shown in figure 7.2. Use the ROMANS2 text style created in Assignment #1 for the parts list body. Use MC justification for the NO column, and ML justification for the remaining columns.

3. Use the ROMANS3 text style for the heading.

NO	LAYER	NAME
		PARTS LIST
1	RES1	Resistor: .5 W
2	DIODE1	Diode: 1N914
3	DIODE2	Diode: 1n4001 – 1n752A
4	ECAPC1	Elec. Cap.: 10uf 35V
5	DIODE3	Diode: 1N5402
6	ECAPC2	
7	ICU1	
8	CON1	
9	REG1	
10	CAPC4	.01uf
11	TRANSQ1	
12	WIRE1	
13	ICU2	LM741 – lf735 Op-Amp
14	REG2	
15	REG3	7805-lm317-lm337
16	REG4	
17	ECAPC3	Elec. Cap.: 1000uf 35V

Figure 7.2 *Create the parts list for use in a printed circuit board.*

Unit 7 Assignment #3

1. Open the PCB drawing and create the following layers:

Layer	Component Name	Color	Linetype
ECAPC3	Electronic Capacitor (1000uf 35V)	220	Continuous
ECAPC2	Electronic Capacitor (2200uf 35V)	221	Continuous

2. Draw the capacitors shown in figure 7.3. The capacitor on the top is ECAPC3.

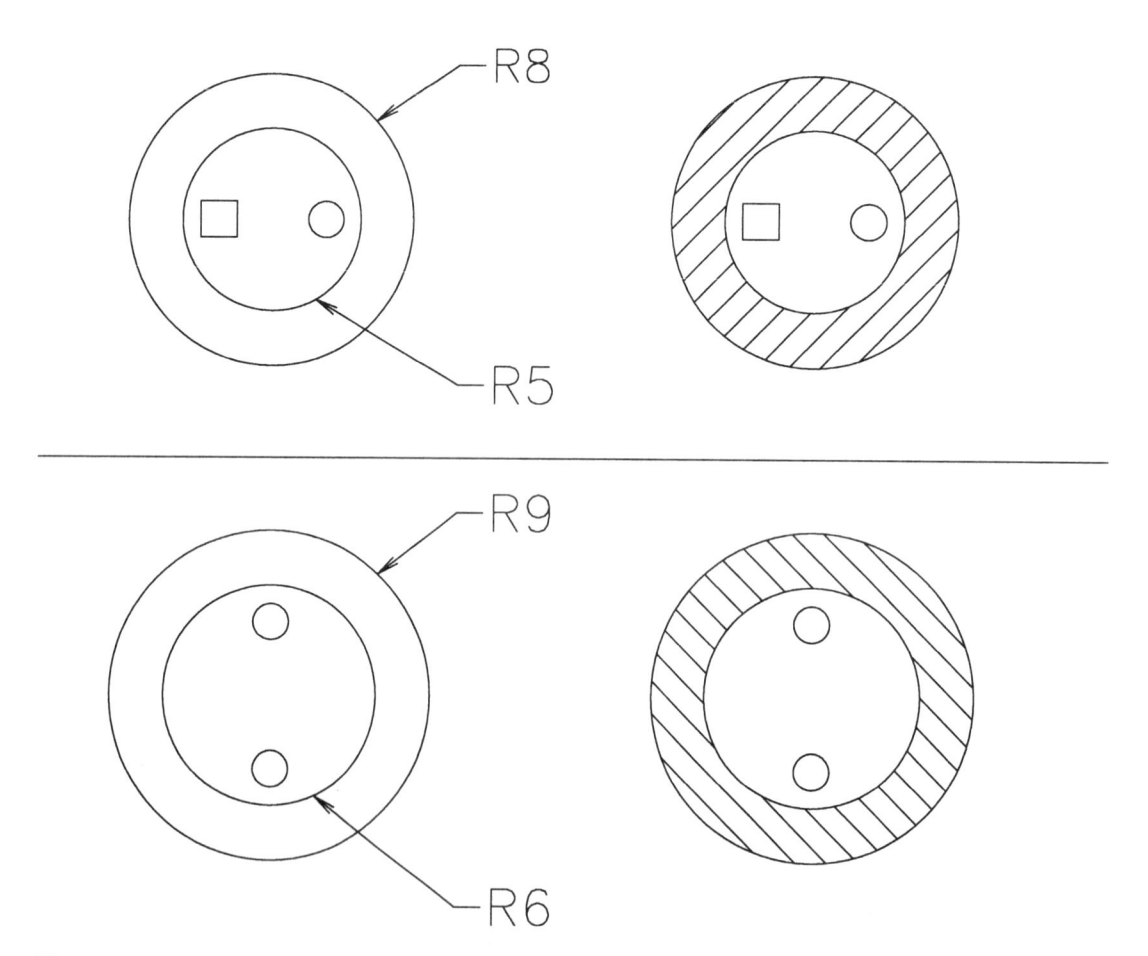

Figure 7.3 *Create the capacitors on the PCB drawing.*

Unit 7 Assignment #4

1. Open the MDEFAULT drawing as a template and create the following layers:

Layer	Component Name	Color	Linetype
BORDER	PCB Border	Magenta	Continuous
HATCH	PCB Hatching	Cyan	Continuous

2. Increase the limits to 250, 230.

3. Draw and hatch the printed circuit board shown in figure 7.4. Begin the lower left corner of the drawing at 15,90.

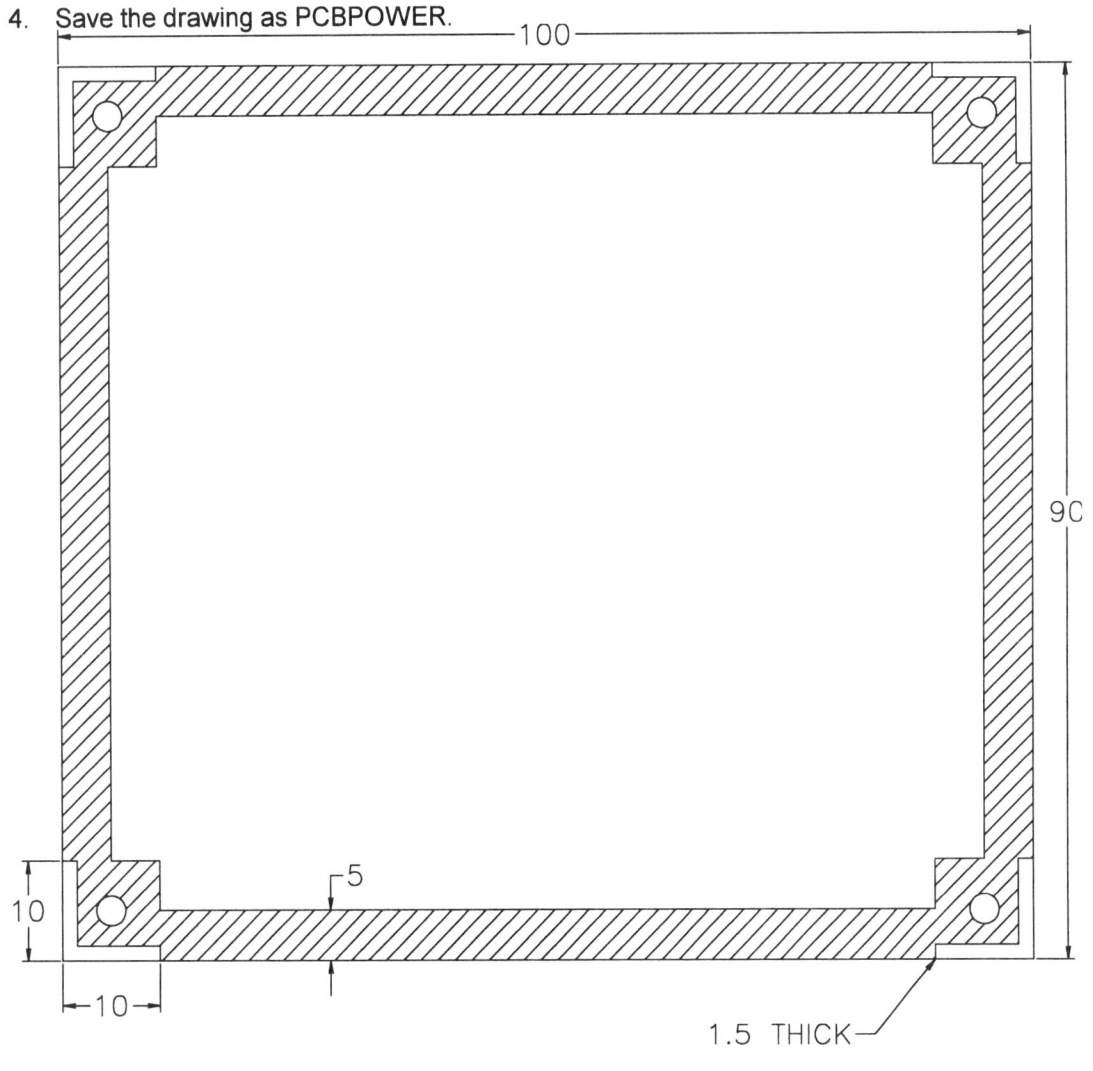

4. Save the drawing as PCBPOWER.

Figure 7.4 *Draw and hatch the printed circuit board.*

Unit 8: Drawing Accurately

Overview

The snap and grid is a fast and accurate method of locating an exact position when creating geometry. Most objects, however, will not line up accurately on the grid, or will have point locations you cannot easily find. The object snap functions allow you to *precisely* locate a specific point on existing objects. The object snap is a tool that will allow you to create drawings quickly and accurately.

Objectives

- Understand the importance of maintaining the integrity of the database and geometry.
- Identify when to use object snaps to locate points on an existing electronics drawing.
- Use QUADrant, ENDpoint and PERpendicular to create electronics symbols.

Introduction

Two important characteristics all CAD drawings must have are:

1. **Integrity of the database**. All information you enter into the CAD system is stored in a database. In AutoCAD, this database is accurate to 14 decimal places. When you are creating geometry, an accurate drawing is extremely important for several reasons. Geometry created on a CAD system is often used more than once. The object may be plotted, used to create the artwork for a printed circuit board, or used to calculate a parts list.

2. **Integrity of the geometry.** When creating geometry, make sure you do not draw lines, arcs, or circles on top of each other. Additionally, a line extending between two points should be just that - a single line, not two short lines connected together. Objects on top of each other may not be readily apparent when viewed on screen or when plotted, but definitely affect the integrity of the geometry. Errors in the final artwork are common when the geometry was not created correctly.

Object snap is simply another tool available to the CAD operator that will increase productivity and accuracy, and maintain the integrity of the database and geometry. Although these tools do not *have* to be used when you create geometry, you will find that with a little practice they will greatly increase your drawing productivity and accuracy.

Section 1: Working with Entity Points and Object Snap

In the main text, object snaps were introduced along with a thorough explanation. In this section of the workbook, we will examine the use of object snaps on a typical electronics symbol. We will use the fuse symbol shown in Figure 8.1 as a case study. This drawing was also created in Unit 6, Creating Basic Geometry. When the symbol was created in Unit 6 you used coordinate entry to locate the points for the line, arcs, and circles. As you will see from this example, the drawing can also be created with object snaps. The proper use of these tools will speed up creation of the drawing as well as ensure its accuracy.

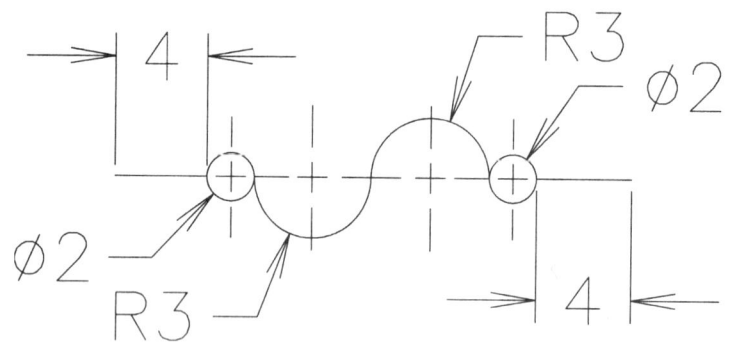

Figure 8.1 *The fuse symbol.*

Examine each use of the Object Snap carefully before moving on. There are many ways to create geometry. See if you can determine another method for creating the same geometry, and what its advantages and disadvantages would be.

Using Various Object Snaps To Create the Fuse Symbol

Object snaps are used to snap to specific locations on *existing* geometry. Obviously the geometry you are snapping to must be accurate. For these examples, we will assume the circle shown in figure 8.2 was created with the correct diameter. The following object snap examples will build upon this geometry.

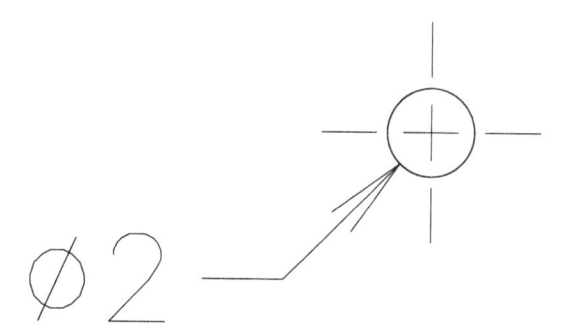

Figure 8.2 *The circle portion of the fuse symbol.*

QUADrant

The first object snap to be discussed is QUADrant. By using the QUADrant osnap, you can locate the endpoint of the line, located at the 180° quadrant of the circle. After snapping to the 180° location on the circle, you can use a relative coordinate by entering @4<180 at the to point: prompt.

QUADrant can also be used on the same circle to locate the start position of the first arc. If the Start, Center, End arc option was used, use the QUADrant object snap to locate the start point of the arc. Since the radius of the arc is given, use relative coordinates to locate the center and endpoints. The relative coordinate for the center point would be @3<0, and @3<0 again for the endpoint.

ENDpoint

The next object snap to be discussed is ENDpoint. It is one of the most widely used snapping functions since it will snap to the exact endpoint of a line or arc. Provided your existing geometry is accurate, using ENDpoint to draw a line between two existing objects can be much quicker than other methods.

Examine figure 8.3. The circle on the right side needs to be created. Using the Circle 2 point option, you can use ENDpoint object snap to locate the end of the arc. When prompted for the second point, enter a relative or relative polar coordinate to locate the second point on the circle. When using the ENDpoint osnap to locate the end of the arc, it not only defines the first point on the circle but sets the LASTPOINT system variable. When prompted for the second point on the circle, the relative or relative polar coordinate is based on the LASTPOINT system variable.

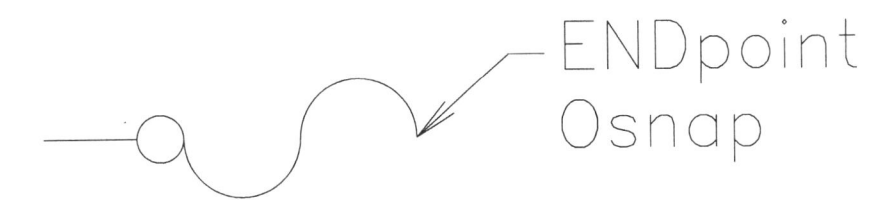

Figure 8.3 *Locating the first point of the circle using ENDpoint object snap.*

PERpendicular

The PERpendicular osnap locates a point on a line, arc, or circle that forms a perpendicular from the current point. This can be very handy, especially when creating schematic drawings. Figure 8.4 shows a schematic drawing of a simple electronics circuit. The wiring lines are thicker to show where the symbols end and the wiring begins. A variety of object snaps are located to indicate where the object snaps could be used to line up the symbols and wiring lines.

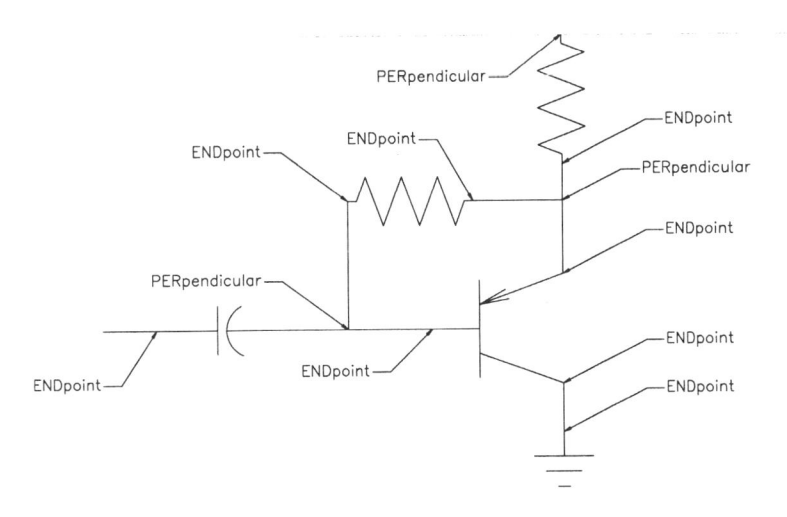

Figure 8.4 *A schematic diagram, with possible object snap points indicated.*

Name _____

Unit 8 Review

1. AutoCAD is accurate to _____ decimal places.

2. The two important characteristics all CAD drawings must have are _____ and _____.

3. When using the CENter object snap, the aperture must touch _____ on the circle.

4. A point object in AutoCAD is referred to as a _____.

5. When using the QUADrant object snap mode, you can find the _____, _____, _____, and _____ degree locations on a circle.

6. The location point where text was initially created is called its _____.

7. The temporary object snap mode is effective for _____ selections.

8. The running object snap mode is effective for _____ selections.

9. The box that appears on-screen when object snap modes are used is called the _____.

10. In 2D drawings, the Z coordinate is always _____.

77

Unit 8 Assignment #1

1. Open the PCB drawing and create the regulator symbols shown in figure 8.5.

2. Create the layers shown below.

3. Use the dimensions given in figure 8.5 as a guide when creating the symbols. To ensure accuracy, use any combination of snap, grid, coordinate entry, and object snaps.

Layer	Component Name	Color	Linetype
REG3	Regulator	45	Continuous
REG4	Regulator	33	Continuous

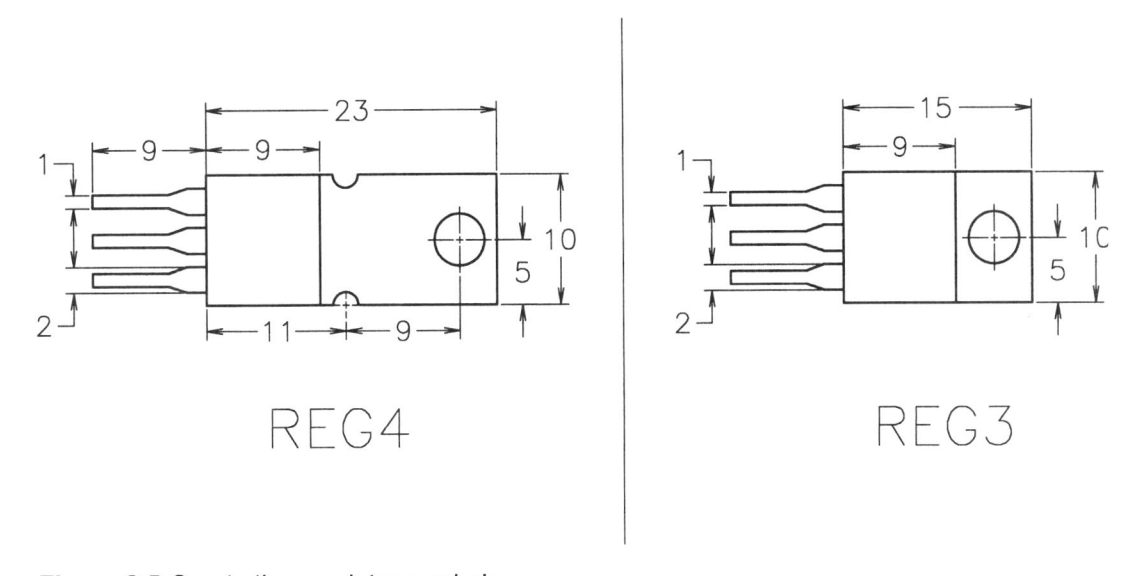

Figure 8.5 *Create the regulator symbols.*

Unit 8 Assignment #2

1. Create a new drawing called COLPITTS, using the SCHEMATIC drawing as a prototype.

2. Use the symbols you created in the SCHEMATIC drawing to draw the Colpitts Oscillator, shown in figure 8.6.

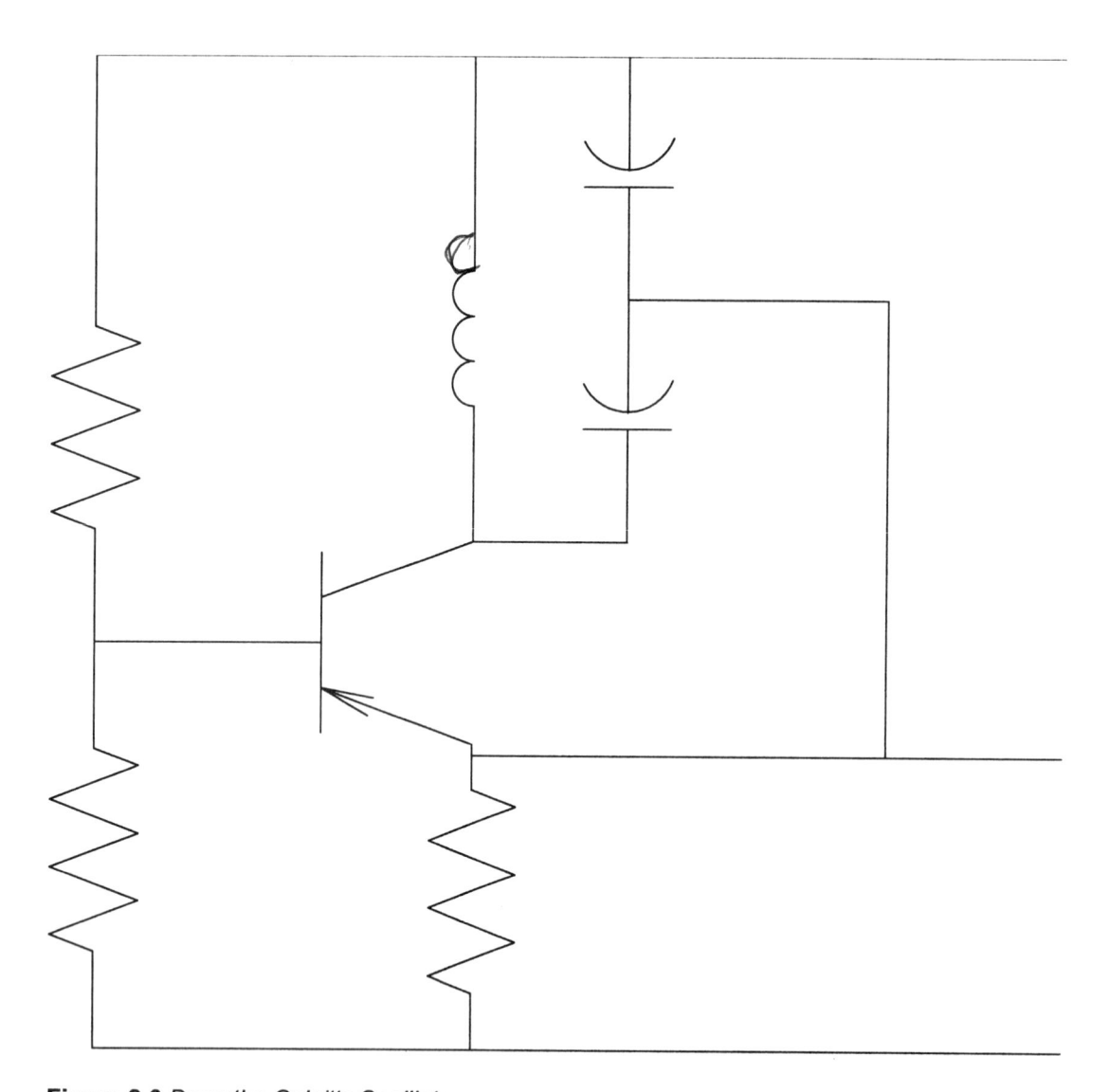

Figure 8.6 *Draw the Colpitts Oscillator.*

Unit 8 Assignment #3

1. Create a new drawing called TICKLER, using the SCHEMATIC drawing as a pro

2. Use the symbols you created in the SCHEMATIC drawing to draw the Tickler, shown in figure 8.7.

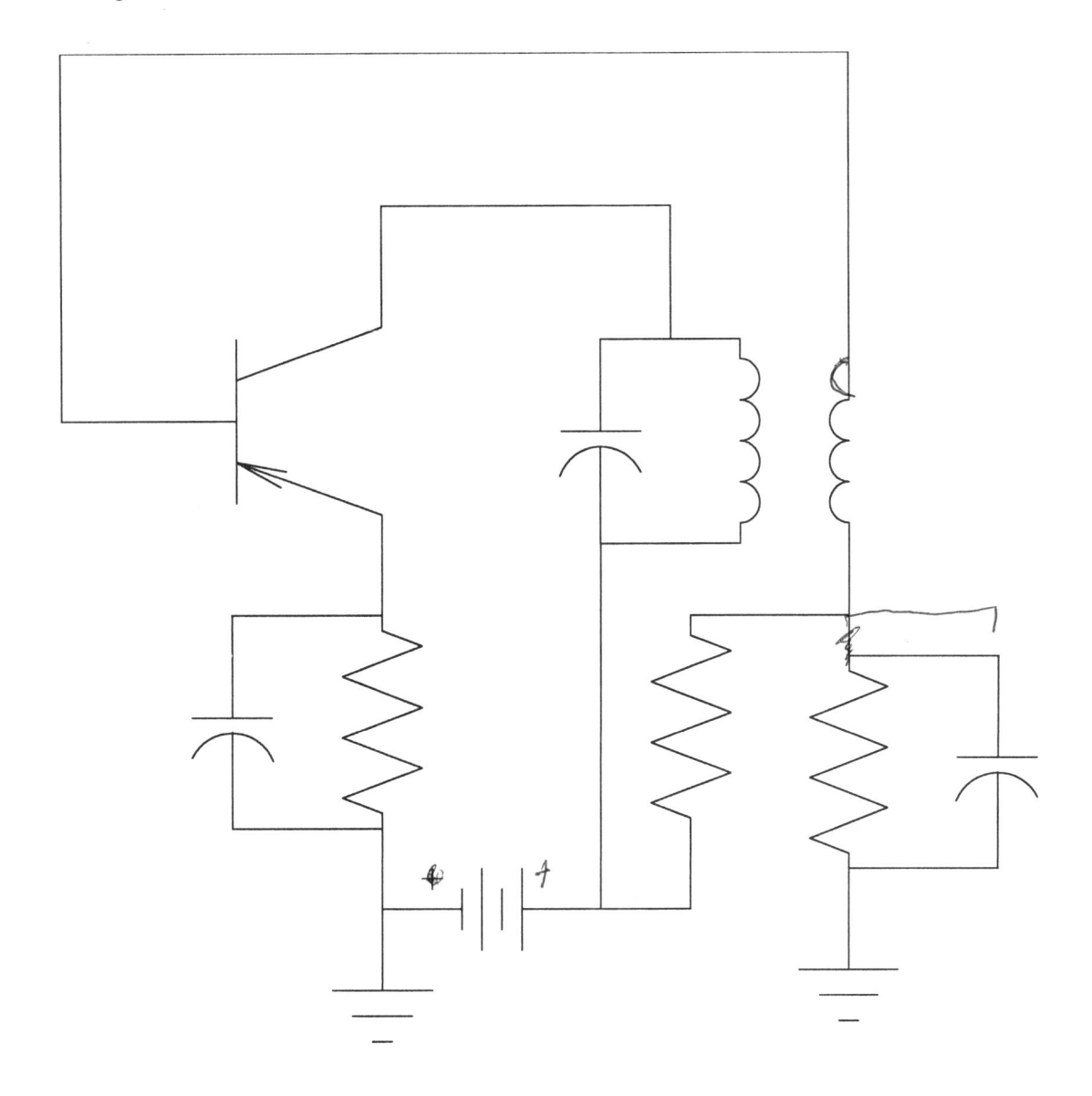

Figure 8.7 *Draw the Tickler.*

Unit 9: Creating Selection Sets

Overview

Selection sets are useful in a variety of situations. During electronic drawing creation they are instrumental in modifying existing objects as well as in the creation of new objects. Another command, GROUP, is very useful for the selection of multiple objects. As this command is introduced, its usefulness to electronic drawings will become apparent.

Objective

- Understand the use of the GROUP command.

Introduction

As was presented in the main text, selection sets allow objects to be selected so that they may be modified, moved, copied, etc. One disadvantage of selection sets is that after they are used, there is no way to make the same selection again later without going through the same lengthy procedures. The GROUP command allows that problem to be overcome.

Section 1: Methods for Creating Selection Sets

Creating selection sets with multiple objects can be a lengthy and time-consuming process. It can be especially frustrating to create a selection set, perform a command on that selection set, and then find that the results are not what was expected or needed. Then the selection set must once again be created, and hopefully the results will be successful on the second attempt. A handy command that can alleviate this problem is the GROUP command. Using this command, a selection set can be created, named, and then saved for later use.

The GROUP Command

Before the GROUP command can be used, a thorough understanding of selection sets must be attained since selection sets are used to create groups. Groups are selection sets that have been created and saved. This command will be very useful for a selection set that contains a large number of objects. Using the following method can access the GROUP command:

- Type GROUP at the command prompt.

Once the command is entered, the Object Grouping dialog box appears as shown in figure 9.1, and the following options are presented:

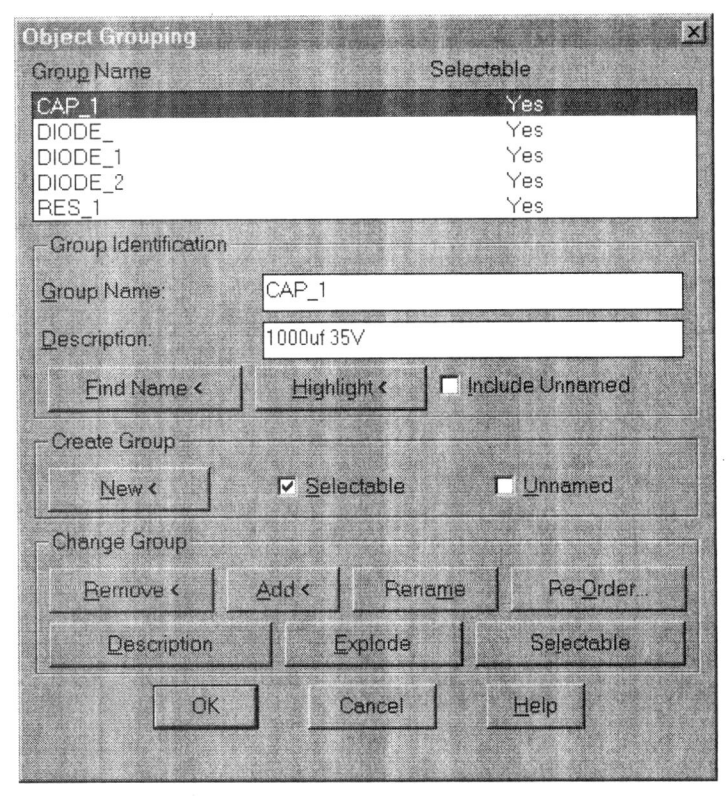

Figure 9.1 *The Object Grouping dialog box.*

- **Group Name.** Enter a group name. The group name convention is the same as layer naming conventions. Once the name is entered, it will be converted to uppercase and that name will be placed in the Group Name listing. Be sure to give the group a meaningful name. Examples of good names are shown in figure 9.1.

- **Description.** Enter a descriptive phrase for the group. The description can be up to 64 characters long. Although optional, it may assist in identifying groups that have been created earlier and are not easily identified by the name. An example description is found in figure 9.1.

- **Find Name.** Allows an object to be selected and then lists the name of the group or groups to which that object belongs.

- **Highlight.** Shows all objects within a group. When this option is selected the groups are displayed within the drawing area and the dialog box shown in figure 9.2 is displayed. Once the objects have been reviewed, select the Continue button on the Object Grouping dialog box prompt as shown in figure 9.2.

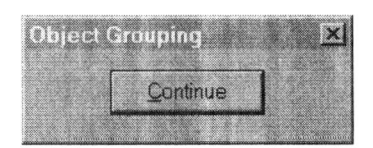

Figure 9.2 *Once the group has been highlighted and reviewed select the Continue button.*

83

- **Include Unnamed.** Allows unnamed groups to be displayed in the dialog box. On occasion, groups without names are created. They are given an arbitrary name. Avoid creating groups without names.

- **New.** Creates a new group. In order to create a new group, a name must first be placed in the Group Name text edit box. Then, selecting the New button will return you to the drawing area. Select the objects to be included in the group using selection set techniques. Once the objects have been selected, right click. The Object Grouping dialog box will return and the group will be listed in the Group Name listing.

- **Re-Order.** Selecting this button will display the Order Group dialog box as shown in figure 9.3. This dialog box is used to change the order of the objects within the group. Objects are numbered as they are selected into the group. This option is rarely needed, so this text will not discuss the options in detail. Consult the AutoCAD Reference for more information if this option is needed.

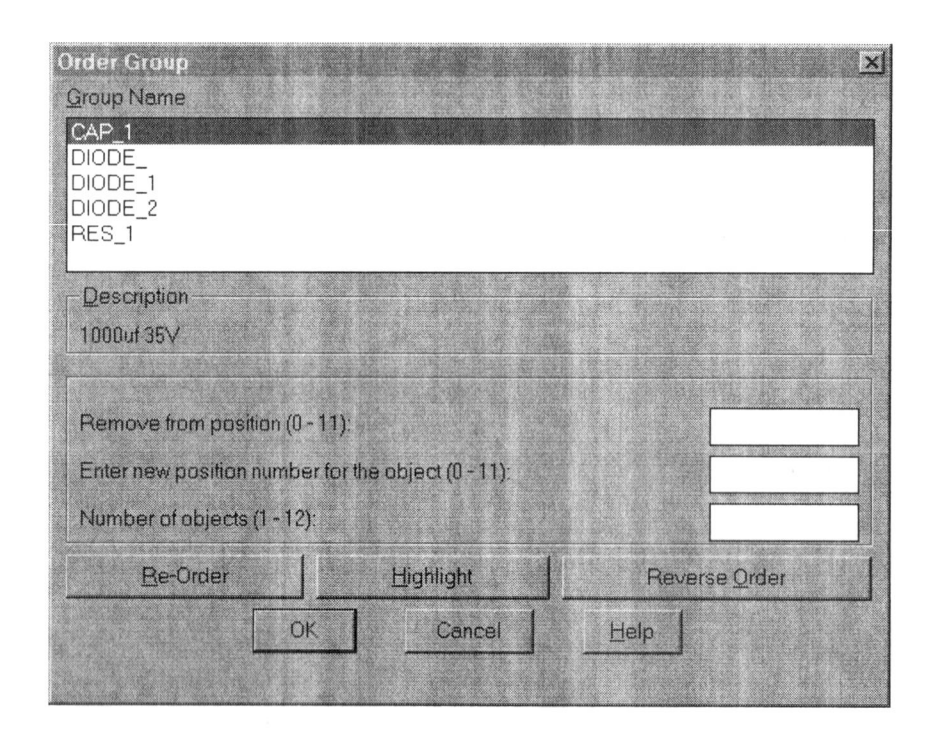

Figure 9.3 *The Order Group dialog box.*

- **Description.** Changes the existing description of a group. Use the procedures outlined for Rename.

- **Explode.** Deletes a group. Select the group to be deleted from the Group Name text edit box and then select the Explode button. The group definition is deleted from the list. The objects will remain in the drawing.

- **Selectable.** Specifies whether a new group being created is selectable. The status of the group will be displayed in the Selectable list. The two options are Yes (selectable) or No (not selectable). If a group is selectable, selecting any object within the group will select the entire group. If a group is not selectable, each individual object can be selected without selecting the rest of the group.

- **Unnamed.** Creates a group without a given name. AutoCAD assigns an anonymous name, *AN, where N is a sequential number that indicates the new number of unnamed groups as they are created. As mentioned, this is not recommended.

- **Remove.** Removes objects from a group. All objects can be removed from a group and that group will remain. When an object is removed from the group it is not removed from the drawing.

- **Add.** Adds objects to a previously defined group.

- **Rename.** Renames a selected group. To rename a group, select the group to be renamed, enter a new name in the Group Name text edit box, and then select the Rename button.

Consider using groups to assist in moving or copying large groups of symbols. As you begin to use groups you will find many uses for them and they will soon be a regular tool in your AutoCAD toolbox.

Name _____

Unit 9 Review

1. Give two examples of when it might be beneficial to use the GROUP command: _____ and _____.

2. _____ are used to group objects together in named selection sets.

List five methods for selecting objects.

3. _____

4. _____

5. _____

6. _____

7. _____

8. True or False. Exploding a group will remove the objects within that group from the drawing area.

9. True or False. Holding the s is necessary while selecting objects to be included in a selection set.

10. True or False. Once objects are added to a selection set, they can be removed before a command is processed.

Unit 9 Assignment # 1

In this assignment you will create the digital symbols found in figure 9.4. Follow the directions below to assist in the creation of this drawing.

1. Create a new drawing named *Digital Symbols*.

2. Set up a drawing for a U.S. Customary A-size sheet of paper.

3. Set SNAP = .125 and GRID = .125.

4. Create one of each of the digital symbols found below. Use the grid to assist in sizing the symbols.

5. Once each symbol has been created, create the groups below with their descriptions. If you are unsure as to which symbol is which, consult a digital electronics book or ask your instructor for assistance.

6. Ensure that layers, linetypes, and colors are used.

7. Add your name or a title block to the drawing.

8. Save the drawing. You will use these symbols in an exercise in the next unit.

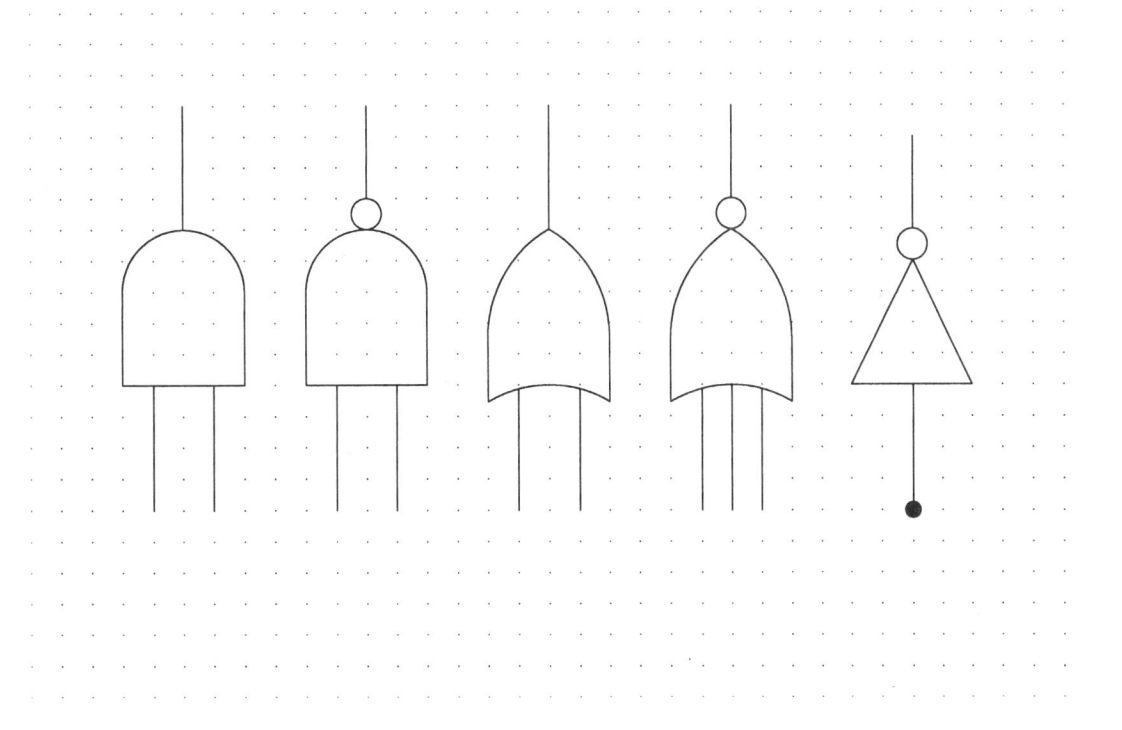

Figure 9.4 *The various digital symbols.*

Unit 10: Basic Editing Skills

Overview

Editing skills are vital to a complete mastery of AutoCAD. Not only do editing commands edit existing objects, but they also aid in the creation of new objects. This unit will introduce various uses of editing commands for the creation of electronics drawings as well as introduce those commands that have their roots in electronics drawing.

Objectives

- Identify when to use basic editing commands to create or modify electronics drawings.
- Understand the use of the FILLET and CHAMFER commands.
- Understand the use of polar arrays to assist in the creation of electronic drawings.

Introduction

As found in the main text, there are many different editing commands. Because of the variety of editing options available, it may not be readily apparent which commands are useful in given situations. In this unit several editing commands will be presented with examples of different electronic components that can be drawn using these basic editing commands.

Section 1: Offsetting, Rotating, Mirroring, Scaling, and Stretching Objects

The main text introduced many new editing commands and gave general, non-discipline specific, examples. In this section of the workbook, each command along with examples of its use in electronics drawings will be presented. We will use the drawing of the AM radio schematic in figure 10.1 as our case study. Studying this drawing and applying editing commands to its creation will no doubt lead to other ideas for the creation of electronic drawing components.

Examine each example carefully before moving on to the next. See if you can determine another use for the editing command.

Using Various Editing Commands to Create Electronics Parts

OFFSET

The first command to be examined is the OFFSET command. The OFFSET command creates a duplicate of an existing object at a specified distance. This command works differently for lines and circles. If a line is offset then a duplicate of that line is created at a specific distance away from the original line. If a circle or arc is offset, a new circle or arc is created concentric (sharing the same center) to the original. This can lead to some very interesting uses for this command. This command is very useful in creating the many connection lines between the components in the AM radio circuit.

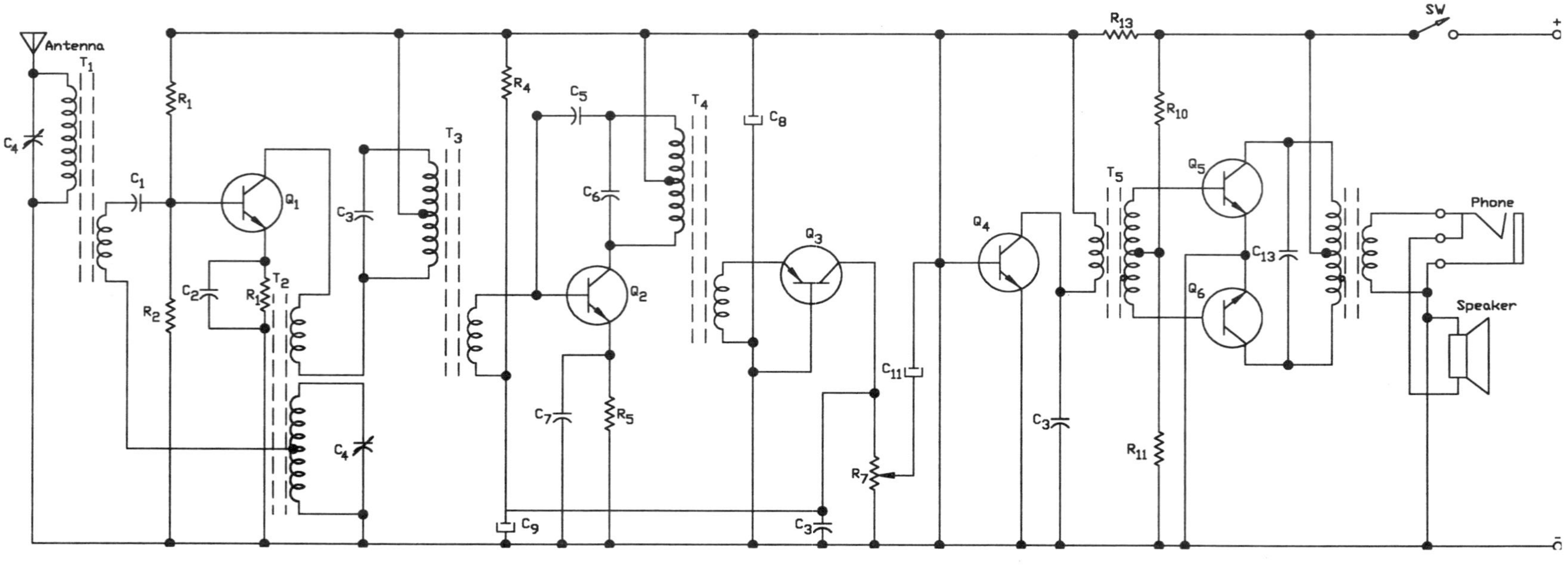

Figure 10.1 Shown above is an example of an AM radio schematic drawing.

ROTATE

The ROTATE command is useful in creating objects in their proper orientation. Examine the resistors R1 and R2. Notice that they are in a vertical orientation. To create R13, R1 can be copied and placed in an approximate location. The ROTATE command can then be used to modify the symbol to a horizontal orientation.

STRETCH

The STRETCH command is useful in modifying connection lines between components that may be too short or too long. It may also be used to modify existing components to correct appearances.

MIRROR

Examine the transistor Q5. Now examine the transistor Q6. What do you notice about them? They are mirrored symbols. To create Q6 consider creating Q5 and then using the MIRROR command to place Q6.

SCALE

Use of the SCALE command is beneficial if a symbol or object is to be enlarged or reduced in size. The antennae symbol in this example could stand to be enlarged so that it is more distinguishable.

Section 2: Editing Edges and Corners of Objects

Two commands provided in AutoCAD have their roots in electronic manufacturing processes. They are the FILLET and CHAMFER commands. Their use and origin are briefly described in this section.

The FILLET Command

The FILLET command will automate the creation of fillets, internal corners, and rounds, external corners. A fillet and a round are generally the by-product of the casting manufacturing process. Parts created during the casting process do not receive sharp corners because the molten metal will deform or destroy the sharp edges of the mold, and molten metal that cools will usually crack around the intersection of two right angle surfaces. A fillet and round usually indicate a part has not been machine finished.

Since the casting process is very common, AutoCAD provides the FILLET command to create representations of these rounded corners. Typically the corner is created square and then the FILLET command is used to round the corner. AutoCAD will also fillet arcs and circles. This allows for some very interesting geometric construction.

The CHAMFER Command

A chamfer is very similar to a fillet, but instead of rounding, it bevels a corner. A chamfer is usually a machined feature and may be found on the ends of cylindrical parts, a connection between two square lines, or a countersunk hole. The CHAMFER command allows a quick and accurate way of recreating these features.

Section 3: Producing Arrays of Objects

The ARRAY command is very useful in the creation of electronic drawings. Both options, rectangular and polar, create new objects based on an original object. Examples of the use of rectangular and polar arrays are described in this section.

Using Rectangular Arrays to Create a Schematic Representation of an External Thread

One use of a rectangular array is in the creation of schematic representations of external threads. A schematic thread representation is one of three methods used to represent threads. The other two are detailed and simplified. In many instances time does not permit nor is it necessary to spend time creating the detailed representation of threads. Likewise, there are times when a simplified representation is too vague to be used. The schematic representation consists of a single pattern that is replicated along the distance of the thread as shown in Figure 10.2. Simply create one instance of the repeating pattern, then array it about either a column (vertical representation) or row (horizontal representation).

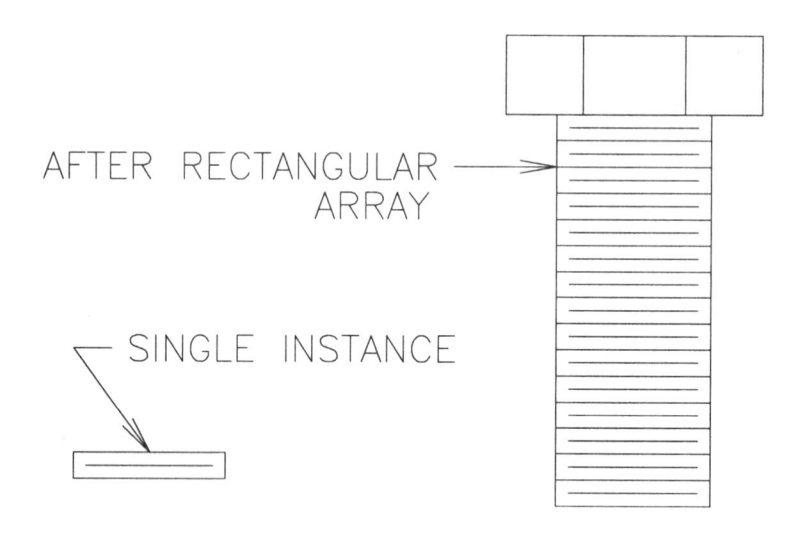

Figure 10.2 *Using a rectangular array to create a schematic thread representation.*

Using Polar Arrays to Create Equidistant Holes

When creating mounts on which circuit boards may be placed, it may be beneficial to create them in a circular pattern about a diameter at points which are equidistant from each other. The polar array will accomplish this task without the need for any layout or math.

Name _____

Unit 10 Review

List the three types of thread representation:

1. _____

2. _____

3. _____

4. A _____ is a rounded exterior corner on a part.

5. A _____ is a rounded interior corner on a part.

6. Rounds and fillets are inherent in the _____ manufacturing process.

7. The _____ command will create a mirrored duplicate of an object.

8. The _____ option of the _____ command is useful in creating objects that are equidistant about a circular path.

9. The _____ option of the _____ command is useful in creating linear duplicates of repeating patterns.

10. Circles that share the same center are referred to as _____.

Unit 10 Assignment # 1

In this assignment you will re-create the drawing of the logic circuit found in figure 10.3. You will use the digital symbols created in Assignment #1 in Unit 9. Follow the directions below to assist in the creation of this drawing.

1. Create a new drawing named *Logic Circuit* using the *Digital Symbols* file that was created in Assignment #1 in Unit 9 as a prototype file.

2. All settings will load from the prototype file so no initial drawing settings will need to be made.

3. Add a .9mm thick border around the drawing.

4. Re-create the drawing shown on the following page. Use the grid to assist in the location of components.

5. As you create the views, try to use modification commands whenever possible to re-create new objects. Remember that the symbols are groups and they can be modified as one object.

6. Ensure that layers, linetypes, and colors are used.

7. Add your name or a title block to the drawing.

8. Plot the drawing at full scale.

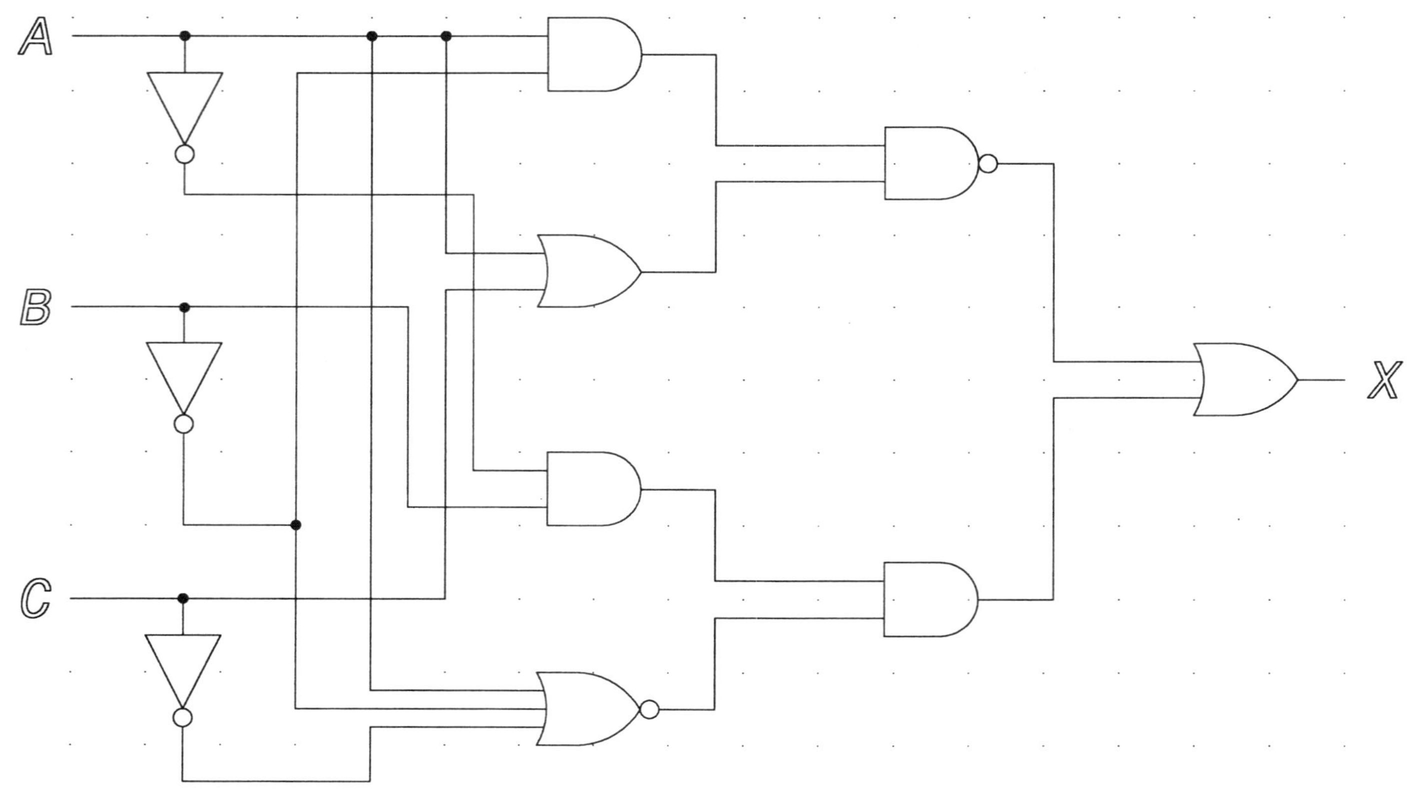

Figure 10.3 *The Logic Circuit drawing.*

Unit 10 Assignment # 2

In this assignment you will create the block diagram and circuit drawing for the crossover network found in figure 10.4. Follow the directions below to assist in the creation of this drawing.

1. Create a new drawing named *Crossover*.
2. Set up a drawing for an A-size sheet of paper. Orient the page vertically (portrait).
3. Set SNAP and GRID to your preferences.
4. Add a .9mm thick border around the drawing.
5. As you create the views, try to use as many modification commands as possible to recreate new objects.
6. Use the GROUP command to assist in the creation of components in the drawing.
7. Ensure that layers, linetypes, and colors are used.
8. Add your name or a title block to the drawing.
9. Plot the drawing at full scale.

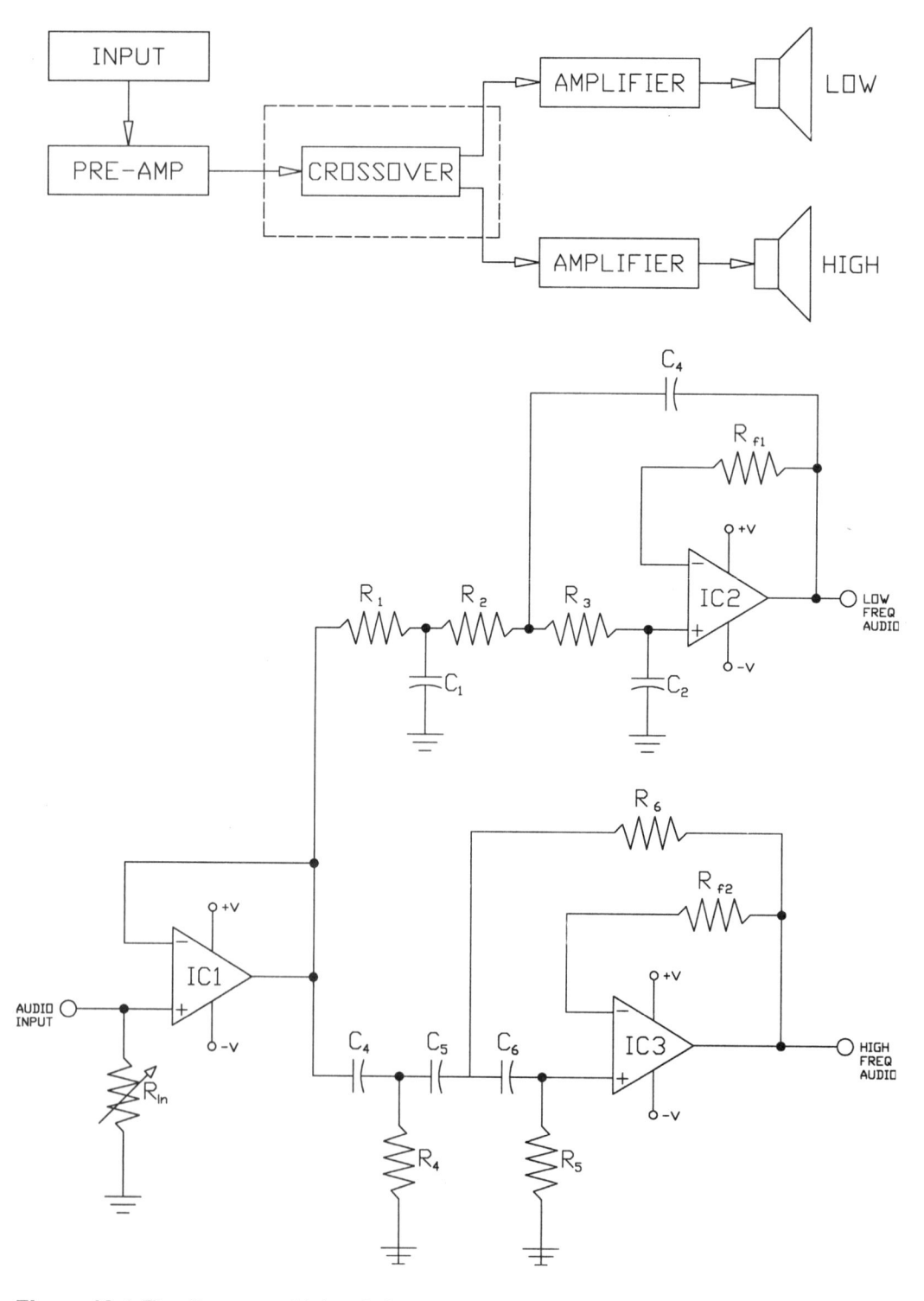

Figure 10.4 *The Crossover Network drawing.*

Unit 11: Editing with Grips

Overview

Grips provide a quick and easy way to modify an individual object. This unit will discuss their use and application as they are applied to electronic drawing.

Objective

- Understand the use of grips to assist in the creation of electronic drawings.

Introduction

In the previous unit the basic editing commands were introduced and a brief explanation of their use in electronic drawing was given. This unit will follow the same format and will present situations where grips may be more advantageous to use than their editing command counterparts.

Section 1: Working with Grips

Grips provide a way to edit objects by displaying small squares or boxes that appear at specific locations on an object. To activate grips, the object must be selected. Once selected you can utilize grip modes such as stretch, move, rotate, scale, and mirror without entering these commands. In this section, examples of their use in electronic drawings will be presented. As in the previous chapter, once an example is presented, a space is provided for you to include additional thoughts about the usage of a grip mode.

Using Grips to Assist in the Creation of Electronics Drawings

It is important to remember that grip modes provide an additional functionality that many of their editing command counterparts do not, such as the ability to edit an object and create a copy of it at the same time. For instance, the grip mode rotate will allow an object to be both rotated and copied. The ROTATE command will only rotate the object.

Stretch

When modifying objects in electronics drafting, it is common to increase the length of a part. The stretch grip mode is very similar to the STRETCH command. It will allow a line to be lengthened or shortened and a circle's diameter to increase or decrease. Another popular use for grips is for making centerlines extend "just a little bit more" past a visible line. The following steps outline the procedure.

1. Select the line.

2. Select the grip on the end of the line that needs to be extended.

3. Move it to the required location.

4. Cancel grips.

Move

The move grip mode is identical to the MOVE command in its operation. It will allow the movement of one or more objects using grips as the base point. Remember that in order to execute this mode you must press the spacebar to cycle through the various grip mode options. Once the objects that are to be moved have been selected, select a grip point as the base point for the move. This mode is useful in moving electronic component symbols.

> **SKILL BUILDER**
> Remember that you can use object snap modes while moving objects to ensure accurate placement.

Rotate

Rotate can be very useful in electronic drawing. Remember that an option of the rotate mode is the ability to not only rotate the object, but also create a copy in the process. This is handy when, for instance, a resistor is needed in another location within a drawing. Using this option, you can copy and rotate an existing resistor symbol into the new location.

Scale

Consider using the scale mode to quickly create scaled equivalents of objects within a drawing. It can be useful for the creation of drawings that contain numerous concentric circles or multiple symbols that are of various sizes.

Mirror

The mirror mode provides features that are almost identical to the MIRROR command except that the default mirror line is created from the grip that is selected. Use this object snap to assist in the creation of symmetrical shapes or in the placement of holes and slots.

> **SKILL BUILDER**
> It is important to remember that grip modes provide an additional functionality that many of their editing commands counterparts do not. For instance the grip mode rotate will an object to be rotated and copied. The ROTATE command will only rotate the object.

> **FOR THE PROFESSIONAL**
> In electronic drafting, the use of grips to modify dimensions can ease dimension modifications significantly. Once the creation of dimensions has been introduced, experiment with the various grip points available on dimensions.

Name _____

Unit 11 Review

1. The _____ command allows the modification of the default grip colors.

2. The _____ command allows the modification of the grip size.

3. Pressing the _____ key will toggle through the available grip modes.

4. The _____ grip mode would be beneficial in the creation of symmetrical shapes.

5. The _____ grip mode is useful in the creation of crossing centerlines.

6. The _____ grip mode can be used to extend or shorten the length of lines.

7. True or False. When rotating objects using the rotate grip mode, rotation points can only be about grips.

8. True or False. Grips can be deactivated.

9. True or False. Grips will modify only one object at a time.

10. True or False. Object snaps cannot be used in conjunction with grips.

Unit 11 Assignment #1

In this assignment you will use grip modes to create the detail drawing of the *Circuit Mounting Guide* found in figure 11.1.

1. Create a new drawing named *Circuit Mounting Guide*.
2. Set up a drawing for an A-size sheet of paper using English units.
3. Set SNAP and GRID to your preferences.
4. Add a .9mm thick border around the drawing.
5. Re-create the views as shown on the following page. You are not required to add the dimensions to the drawing. They are only shown to provide measurements for the part.
6. As you create the views, try to use as many grip modes as possible to re-create new objects.
7. Ensure that layers, linetypes, and colors are used.
8. Create proper centerlines in lieu of creating dimensions.
9. Once the views are created, move them so that they are aligned orthographically and make good use of the space provided.
10. Add your name or a title block to the drawing.
11. Plot the drawing at full scale.

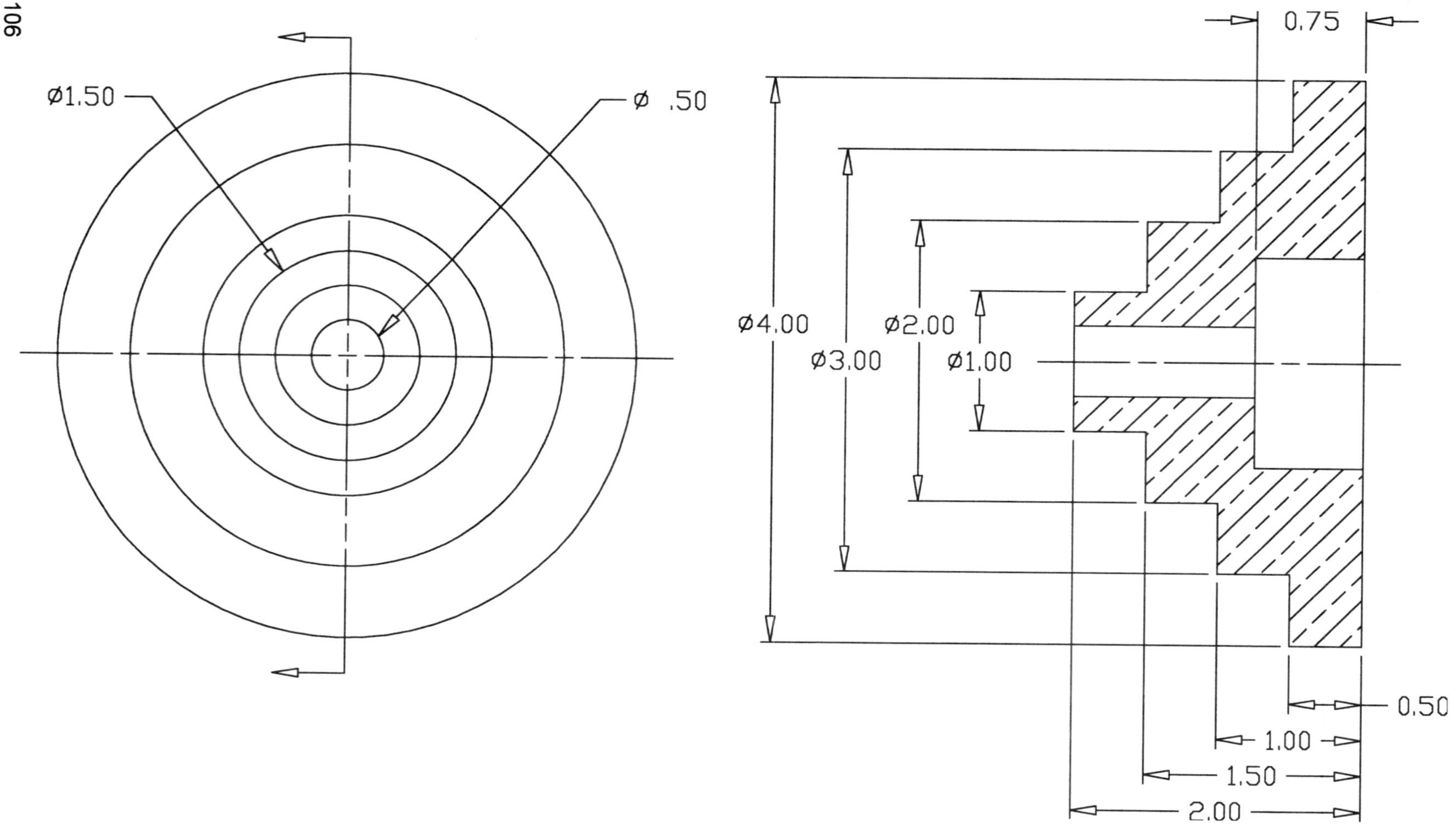

Figure 11.1 *The Circuit Mounting Guide drawing.*

Unit 11 Assignment #2

In this assignment you will use grip modes to create the detail drawing of the *Index Arm* found in figure 11.2.

1. Create a new drawing named *Index Arm*.
2. Set up a drawing for an A-size sheet of paper using English units.
3. This drawing will be plotted at half scale, so ensure that limits are set appropriately.
4. Set SNAP and GRID to your preferences.
5. Add a .9mm thick border around the drawing.
6. Re-create the views as shown on the following page. You are not required to add the dimensions to the drawing. They are only shown to provide measurements for the part.
7. As you create the views, try to use as many grip modes as possible to recreate new objects.
8. Ensure that layers, linetypes, and colors are used.
9. Create proper centerlines in lieu of creating dimensions.
10. Once the views are created, move them so that they are aligned orthographically and make good use of the space provided.
11. Add your name or a title block to the drawing.
12. Plot the drawing at half scale.

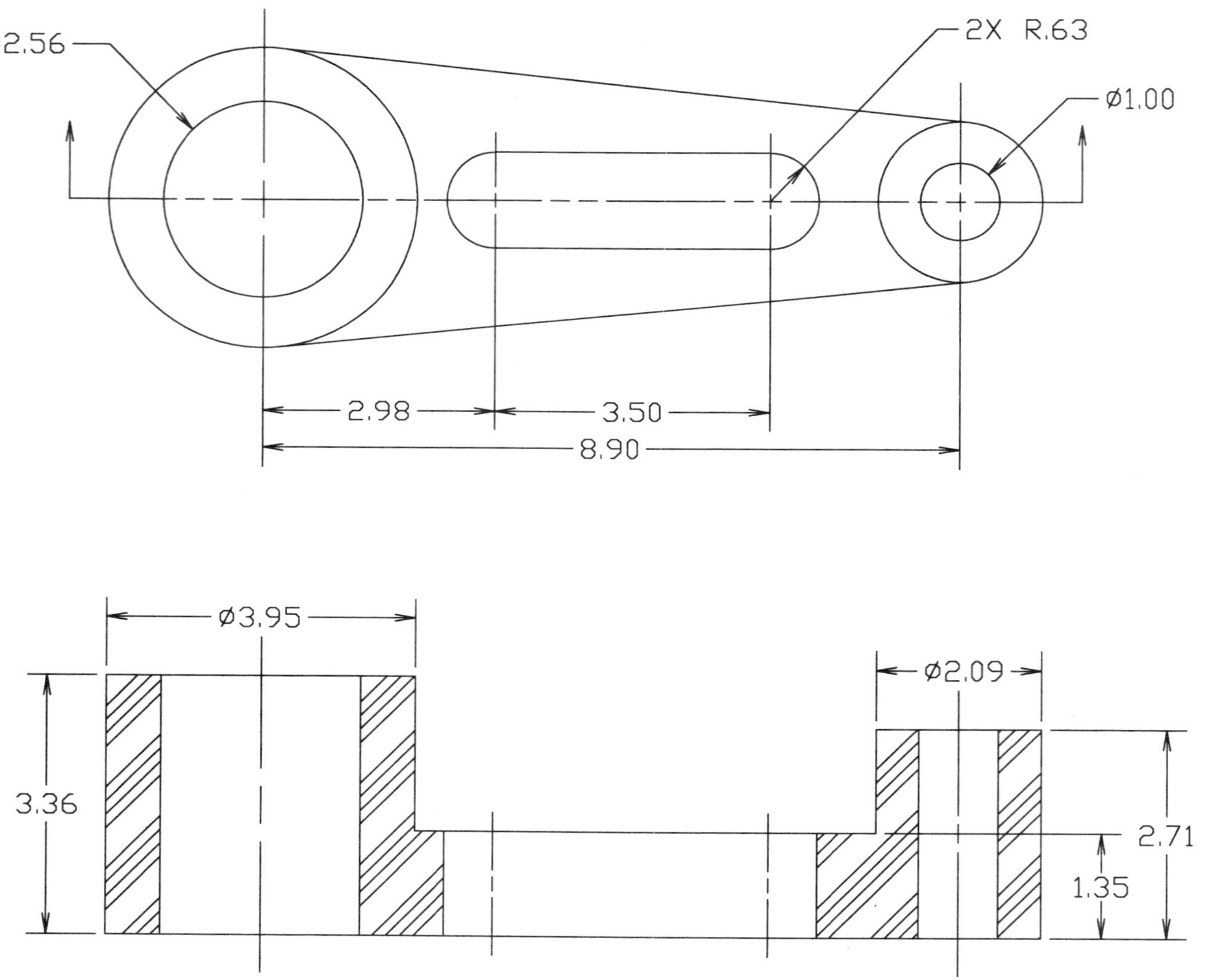

Figure 11.2 *The Index Arm drawing.*

Unit 12: Advanced Drawing Techniques

Overview

In this unit we will look at several additional drawing techniques that can be used to speed geometry creation of different electronic parts.

Objectives

- Use the POINT and MEASURE commands to create a resistor symbol.
- Use the polyline commands to create a printed circuit board.

Introduction

Many electronic drawings contain symbols that are applied at specific intervals in a drawing. By applying the DIVIDE and MEASURE commands, it becomes quite easy to accurately place symbols in a drawing. While there are many different ways to create drawings, the polyline commands can be used to create quickly and accurately lines with different thickness for use in a printed circuit board.

Section 1: Working with POINT and MEASURE to Create a Resistor Symbol

The main text explained the use of the POINT and MEASURE commands and how they can be used to create geometry. The POINT command places points, or nodes on an object. The MEASURE command can be used to place points on an object at specified intervals. When used together, they can simplify the creation of certain electronic symbols. Figure 12.1 shows a typical resistor symbol one might see on a electronic drawing.

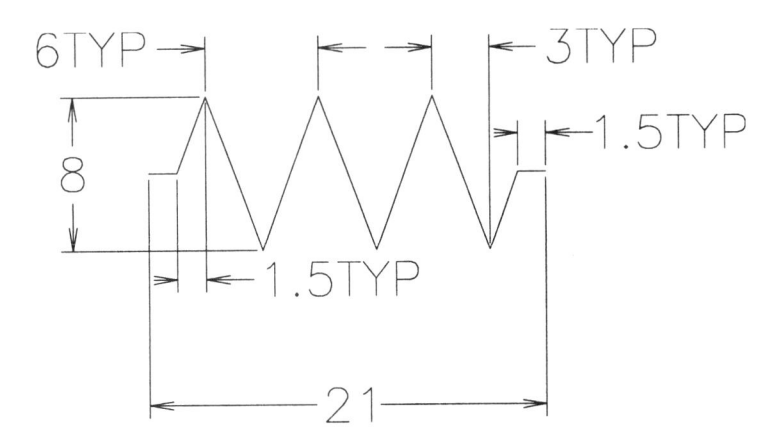

Figure 12.1 *A typical resistor symbol.*

Setting the Point Style and Size

Before using the MEASURE command, you must set the Point Style and Size. By default, points appear as dots on screen. For the resistor symbol example, select the point style that resembles an X, and set the size relative to screen at 5%. The Point Style dialog box should look like figure 12.2. You can access the Point Style dialog box by using one of these methods:

- Enter **ddptype** at the Command: prompt.
- Choose *P*oint Style from the *F*ormat pull-down menu.

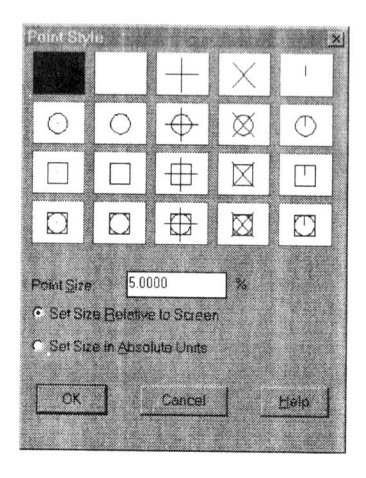

Figure 12.2 *Setting the Point Size and Style used to create the resistor symbol.*

Using MEASURE to Create the Resistor Symbol

Before using the MEASURE command, you have to create some basic geometry to define the outside dimension and the length of the symbol as shown in Figure 12.3. This geometry can be created using the snap and grid, coordinate entry, or offset.

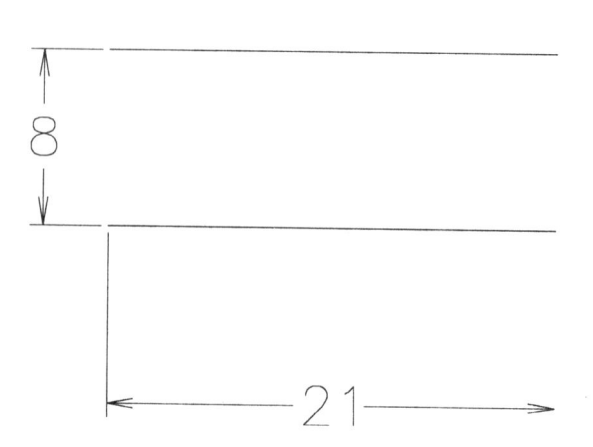

Figure 12.3 *Defining the outside dimension and length of the symbol.*

The next step is to measure the two lines representing the outside diameter into 3mm sections. Using the MEASURE command will place nodes at 3mm intervals on each line, shown in figure 12.4.

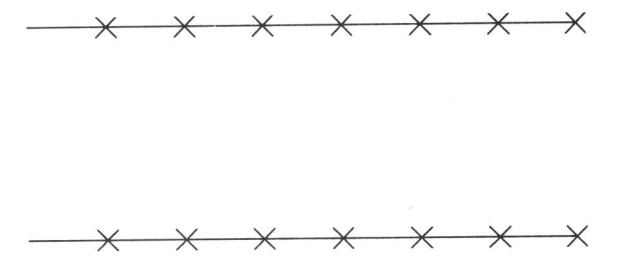

Figure 12.4 *Measuring the outside diameter into 3mm intervals.*

Set a running OSNAP to NODE and ENDpoint, and draw diagonal lines between the points. Draw a line between the end of the bottom line to the first point on the top line, between the first point on the top line and the second point on the bottom line, etc., as shown in figure 12.5.

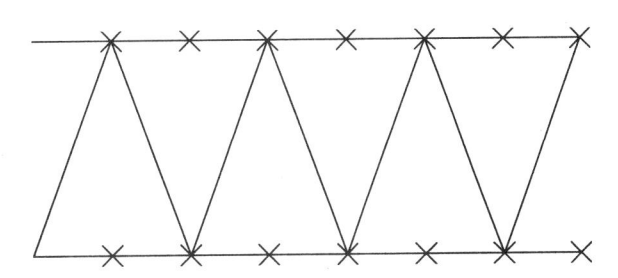

Figure 12.5 *Use the NODE and ENDpoint osnap to draw diagonal lines between points.*

The next step involves drawing the short lines that appear on both ends of the symbol. One method that could be used would be offset. This would involve offsetting either the top or bottom line, then trimming it to the proper length. Another method would use a MIDpoint osnap and the ORTHO mode to draw the short lines, as shown in figure 12.6.

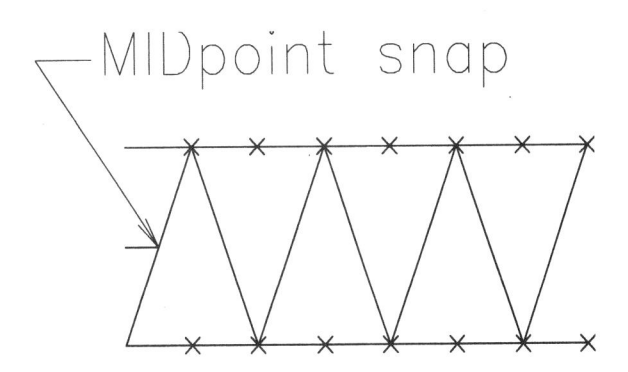

Figure 12.6 *Using MIDpoint osnap and ORTHO mode.*

The final step involves trimming the remaining lines, and either deleting or freezing the construction geometry. The completed resistor symbol is shown before and after trimming in figure 12.7.

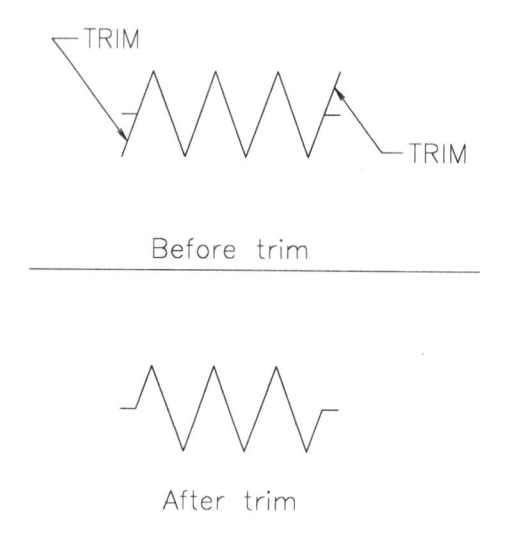

Figure 12.7 *Using the TRIM command to complete the resistor symbol.*

This is only one technique that could be used to draw the resistor symbol. For example, you could also draw one section of the symbol and use the ARRAY command to complete it.

Section 2: Creating IC Pads with DONUT

For laying out printed circuit boards, the DONUT command is very useful for creating IC pads with only one instruction. The DONUT command generates either a circle with a hole in the center (a donut) or a circle that is completely filled in as shown in figure 12.8. When creating these circles, AutoCAD requires you to input the inside and outside diameters of the circles. If the inside diameter is zero, you have a solid circle.

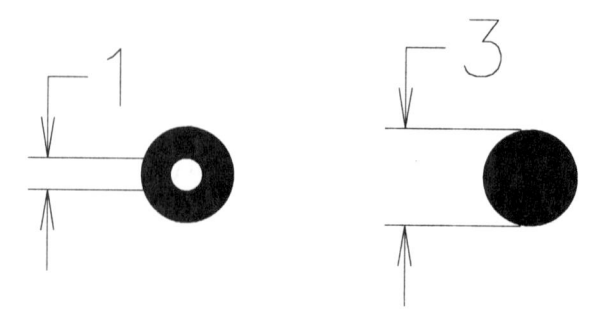

Figure 12.8 *A donut and a solid donut.*

112

Two sizes of donuts commonly used in printed circuit boards are a small size pad, 3 mm in diameter with a 1 mm hole, and a large size pad, 4 mm in diameter with a 1.5 mm diameter hole shown in figure 12.9. You can access the DONUT command by:

- Select Donut from the Draw pull-down menu.
- Enter **donut** or **doughnut** at the Command: prompt.

Large IC Pad

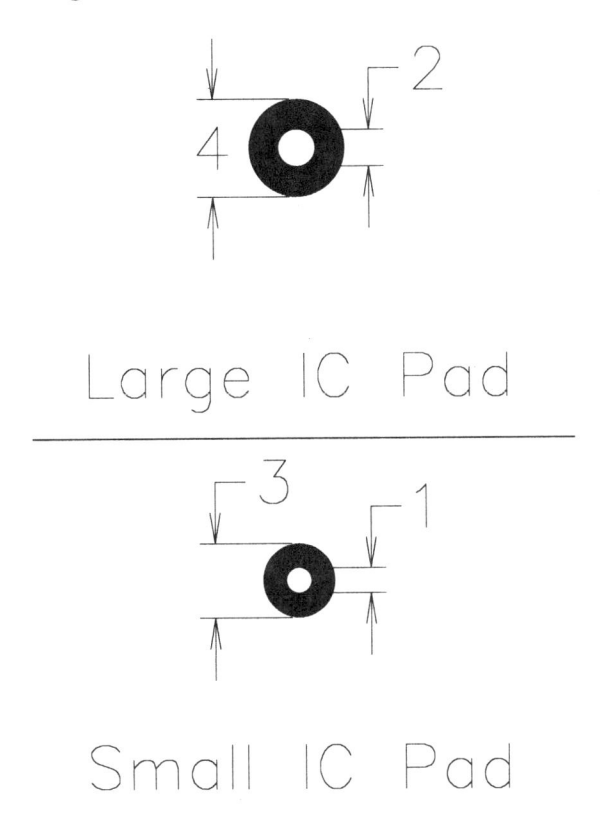

Small IC Pad

Figure 12.9 *The small and large IC pads.*

Section 3: Creating Symbols and PCBs with Polylines

As discussed in the main text, a polyline is a connected sequence of line and arc segments that is treated by AutoCAD as a single entity. A polyline has several special features that make it very useful when creating printed circuit boards. Several features of polylines that make them very useful for electronic drawing are:

- A PLINE can have a specified width, making it ideal for creating the traces that connect components on a printed circuit board.
- PLINE segments can consist of lines and arcs. AutoCAD treats PLINE segments created with one PLINE command as one object. Individual line and arc segments created with the LINE and ARC commands are all individual objects.
- A PLINE can be edited to generate a spline curve. Creating circuit boards with 90° corners can create etching problems during the manufacturing process. Editing a polyline into a spline curve eliminates sharp edges or corners.

- Polylines are very flexible and can be used to draw any shape. This makes it ideal for creating certain symbols, such as diodes.

Creating a Diode Symbol with Polylines

Figure 12.10 shows a general diode symbol. To create the symbol, we will assume the basic geometry is already created as shown in figure 12.11.

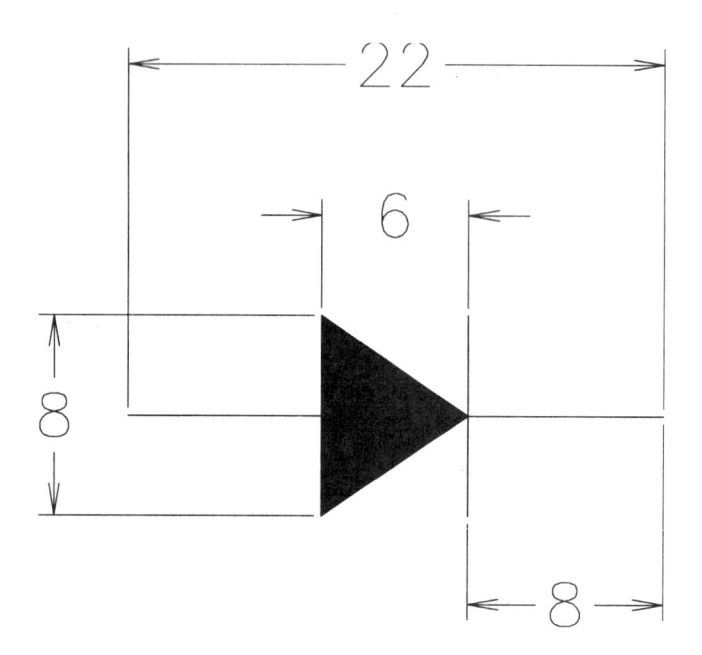

Figure 12.10 *A general diode symbol.*

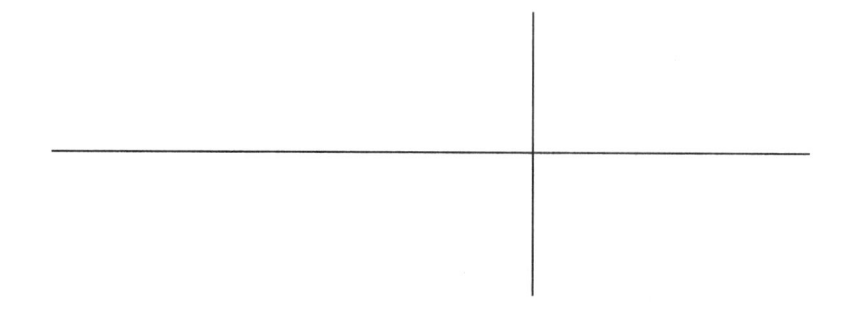

Figure 12.11 *Basic geometry for the diode symbol.*

The following methods can be used to begin the PLINE command:

- Choose the Polyline button from the Draw floating toolbar.
- Type **pline** at the Command: prompt

The PLINE command begins the same as the LINE command. After the start point is established, the PLINE options are accessible. The following command sequence will create the triangular portion of the diode symbol.

```
Command: pline

Specify start point: 18,10

Current line-width is 0

Specify next point or [Arc/Close/Halfwidth/Length/Undo/Width]: h This

will allow you to set the starting width of the polyline.

Specify starting half-width <0>: 4

Specify ending half-width <4>: 0

Specify next point or [Arc/Close/Halfwidth/Length/Undo/Width]: 24,10

Specify next point or [Arc/Close/Halfwidth/Length/Undo/Width]:
```

Turning Fill ON and OFF

By default donuts and polylines appear as solid objects when created. If you have a large number of donuts and polylines on your drawing, they can slow down redraw and regeneration time considerably. If you are outputting to a pen plotter, the amount of time and pens it takes to color in the polylines and donuts is substantial. The FILL system variable controls the display of polylines and donuts. You can access the FILL system variable as follows:

- Enter fill at the Command: prompt.

After changing the FILL variable, issue a REGEN to regenerate the screen and display the polylines and donuts as outlines. Turning FILL OFF will cause the donuts to appear and plot as outlines.

Name _____

Unit 12 Review

1. You can change the size and style of point by accessing the _____ dialog box.

2. By default a point created with the POINT command appears as a _____ on the screen.

3. Setting the point size relative to the screen size causes the points to _____ when you zoom in and out and regenerate the screen.

4. When using the DIVIDE command on an object, it does _____ to the selected object.

5. When using the MEASURE command on an object, it does _____ to the selected object.

6. The MEASURE command can also be used to insert not only points but also _____ in the current drawing at specified intervals.

7. An object created with the PLINE command consisting of two lines and one arc has _____ separate components.

8. The system variable used to change the display and plotting of polylines and donuts is _____.

9. To smooth out the corners in a polyline, use the _____ command, which is considered a PEDIT command.

10. To change an established series of lines and arcs into a polyline, use the _____ command.

Unit 12 Assignment #1

1. Open the PCB drawing and create the symbols shown in figure 12.12.

2. Create the following layers:

Layer	Color	Linetype
DIODE1	40	Continuous
DIODE2	40	Continuous
DIODE3	40	Continuous
ECAPC1	30	Continuous
RES	171	Continuous

3. Use the dimensions given in figure 12.12 as a guide when creating the symbols. To speed up the creation of the symbols, use the RECTANG command.

4. Use a polyline at the end of the symbols with a halfwidth of .5 mm and a length of 5 mm.

DIODE3

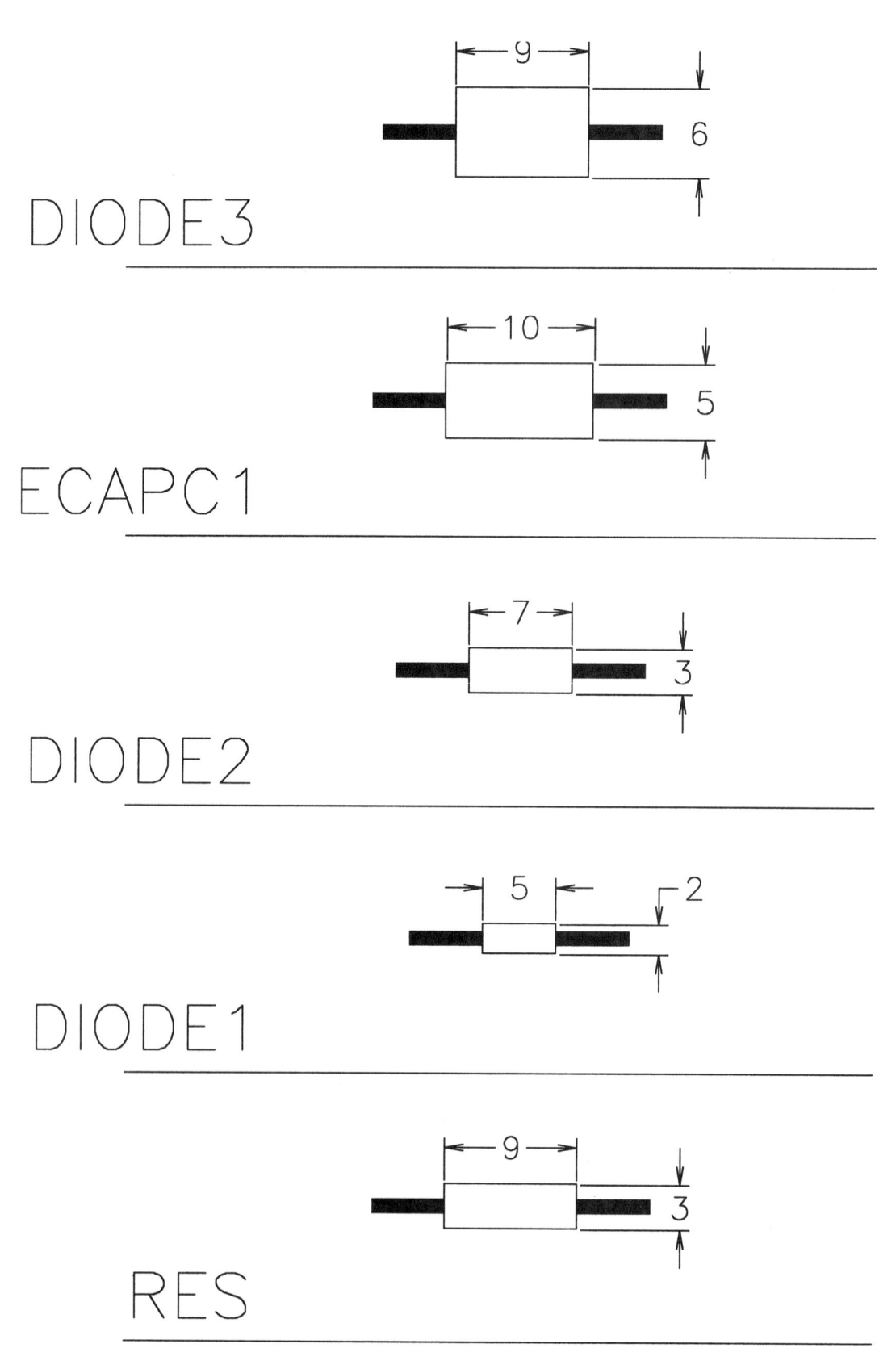

ECAPC1

DIODE2

DIODE1

RES

Figure 12.12 *Create the electronic symbols using a rectangle and a polyline.*

Unit 12 Assignment #2

1. Open the PCB drawing and create the symbols shown in figure 12.13.

2. Create the following layers:

Layer	Color	Linetype
CON1	white	Continuous
ICU1	95	Continuous
ICU2	95	Continuous
WIRE	red	Continuous

3. Use the dimensions given in figure 12.13 as a guide when creating the symbols. Use the DIVIDE command when creating the ICU symbols. The radius of the small circles is .5 mm.

4. Use a polyline at the end of the symbols with a halfwidth of .5 mm and a length of 5 mm.

5. Use the MEASURE or ARRAY command to create the CON1 symbol. The polylines in the symbol have a halfwidth of .5 mm.

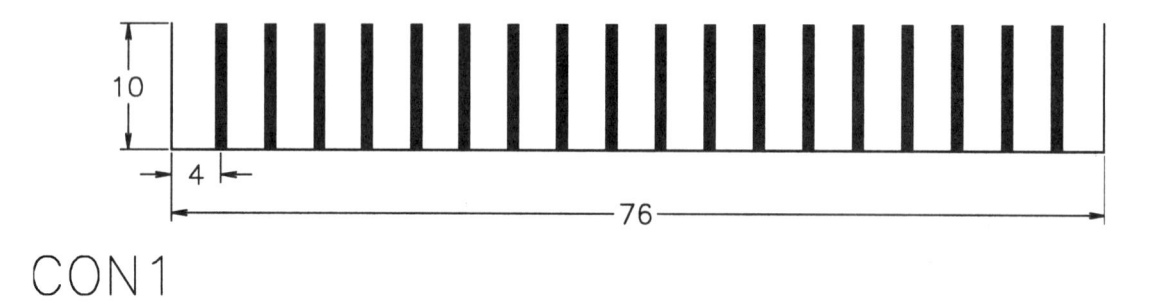

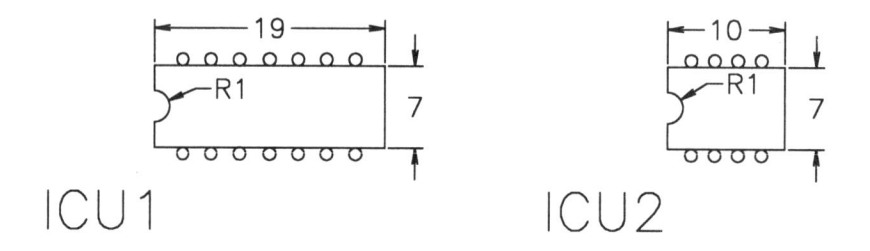

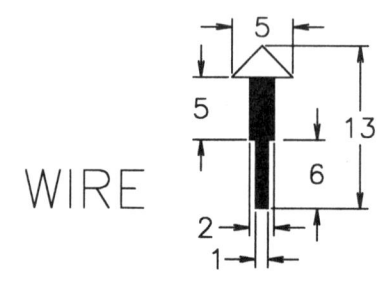

Figure 12.13 *Create the electronic symbols on the PCB drawing.*

Unit 13: Dimensioning a Drawing

Overview

Dimensioning has a unique feel in each of the various disciplines that utilize AutoCAD. In this unit, dimensioning as it relates to electronic drafting will be discussed. This unit begins with an introduction of mechanical dimensioning standards that have been established by ANSI/ASME. A discussion of mechanical standards is very important since electronic drafters in the U.S also follow those standards. After this introduction, the various ways to ensure that these standards are enforced when using AutoCAD will be explained.

Introduction

Dimensioning is perhaps one of the most frustrating tasks for a new AutoCAD user. While AutoCAD does provide many powerful commands, sometimes the plethora of commands is overwhelming to the new student. Add to this the fact that AutoCAD does not inherently adhere to any known standard and that there is still quite a bit of user decision making, AutoCAD can be "down-right stubborn" when it comes to the simplest of dimensions. This unit will address a few of AutoCAD's shortcomings as a dimensioning tool and how to adhere to ASME standards.

Section 1: Dimensioning Basics

In the area of electronic drafting there is one standard, ASME. This organization develops and adopts standards that ensure drawing compatibility among manufacturing organizations. These standards address everything from sheet size to the size of the gap in a hidden line. It is imperative that every electronic draftsperson be familiar with these standards.

ASME Standards

The standards governing the way electronic drawings are created and dimensioned are those adopted by the American National Standards Institute (ANSI) and published by the American Society of Mechanical Engineers (ASME). The current standard is *Dimensioning and Tolerancing, ASME Y14.5M -1994*. This standard was developed in order to ensure compatibility and readability between manufacturing organizations. If this standard is adhered to, all manufacturing organizations can exchange drawings without the fear of interpretation error due to organization-specific techniques and symbology. It is therefore important that these standards are learned early in a career and their use refined over the years.

This unit will complement these standards as much as possible, therefore ensuring that these standards are immediately applied to electronic drawings created in AutoCAD. As you will find in our exploration of these dimensioning standards, many of the AutoCAD default values will have to be changed in order to adhere to these standards. Because of the numerous changes, consider creating a prototype drawing with the settings discussed in this unit.

> **FOR THE PROFESSIONAL**
>
> When creating electronic drawings, try to have a copy of the standards for *Dimensioning and Tolerancing, ASME Y14.5M-1994* available to answer any questions you may have in the course of drawing creation. Need a copy? They can be obtained from:
>
> American Society of Mechanical Engineers
> 345 East 47th Street
> New York, NY 10017
>
> American National Standards Institute
> 1430 Broadway
> New York, NY 10018

The fundamental dimensioning rules that adhere to ASME Y14.5M-1994 standards can be found in figure 13.1 on the following page. This figure will be used as a reference for many of the examples in this unit and can be used to answer the fundamental questions concerning dimensions. It may be handy to make a copy of this figure and keep it by your side until it is memorized. Because not all rules can be covered in this workbook, it would be good to have a copy of the standards available or an engineering drafting book that has been revised to include the updated standards.

Creating Dimension Styles

Dimension styles allow for various dimension settings to be grouped by name. Using these styles can greatly simplify the creation of dimensions. There are two systems that are used to describe objects on an electronics drawing: the United States (US) customary units and the International System of Units (SI). In this section, the dialog boxes that comprise the dimension style will be presented for each system.

United States (US) Customary

The US customary system of units utilizes the inch as the common unit of measure. Used for many years, this system is quickly being replaced by the SI system. It should not as of yet be ignored though. Many drawings exist that use this system and a good many more will be created. Therefore this section will present the settings needed in the Dimension Styles family of dialog boxes. Follow these steps to create a dimension style that conforms to the US customary system.

1. Set the precision of units to 0.0000.

2. Select the Dimension Style button on the Dimensioning toolbar. The Dimension Styles dialog box will be displayed.

3. Create a new style called *US*.

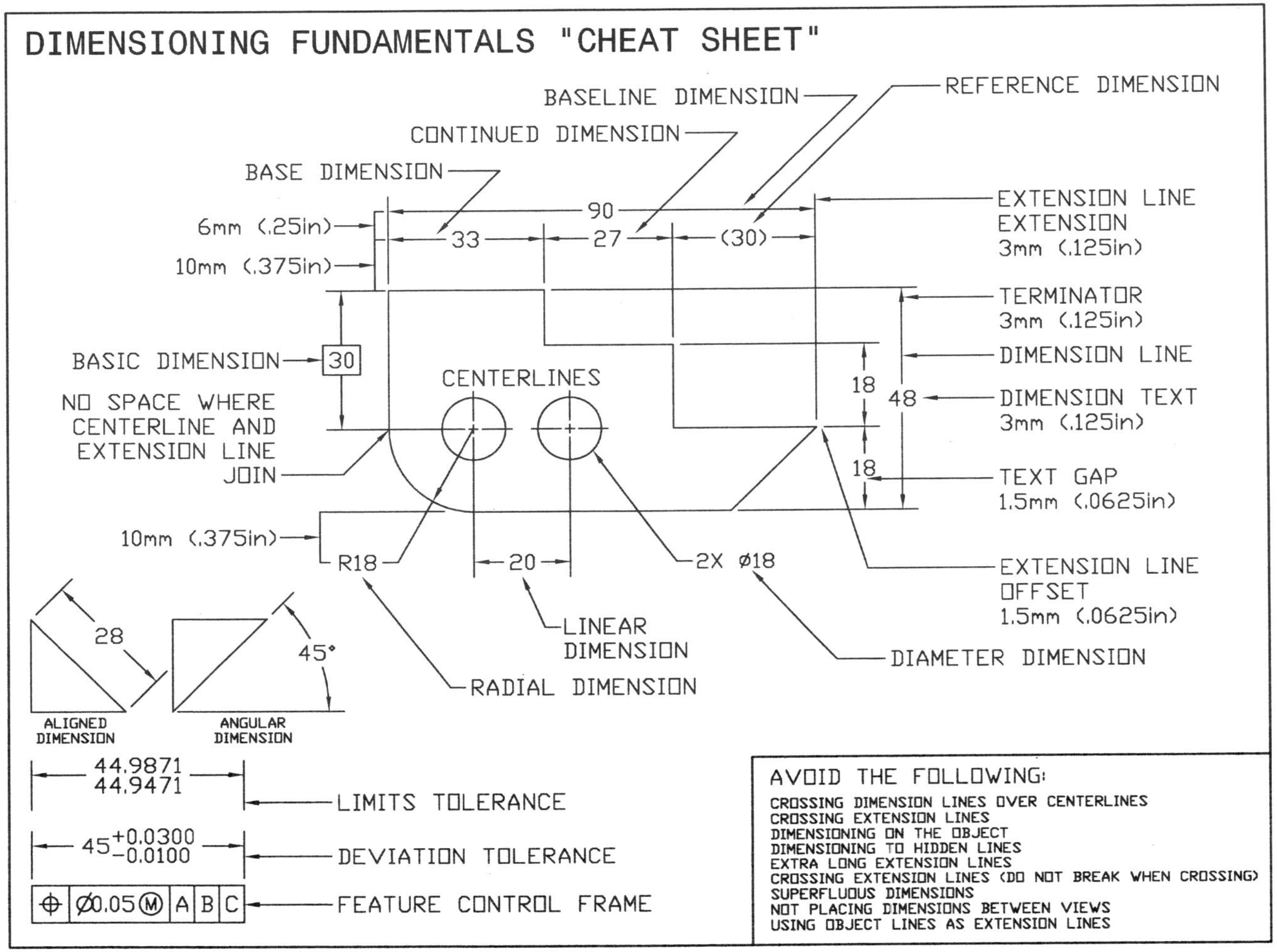

Figure 13.1 *Fundamental rules of dimensioning cheat sheet.*

4. Make sure that the Lines and Arrows tab is selected. Ensure that the settings are the same as those found in figure 13.2.

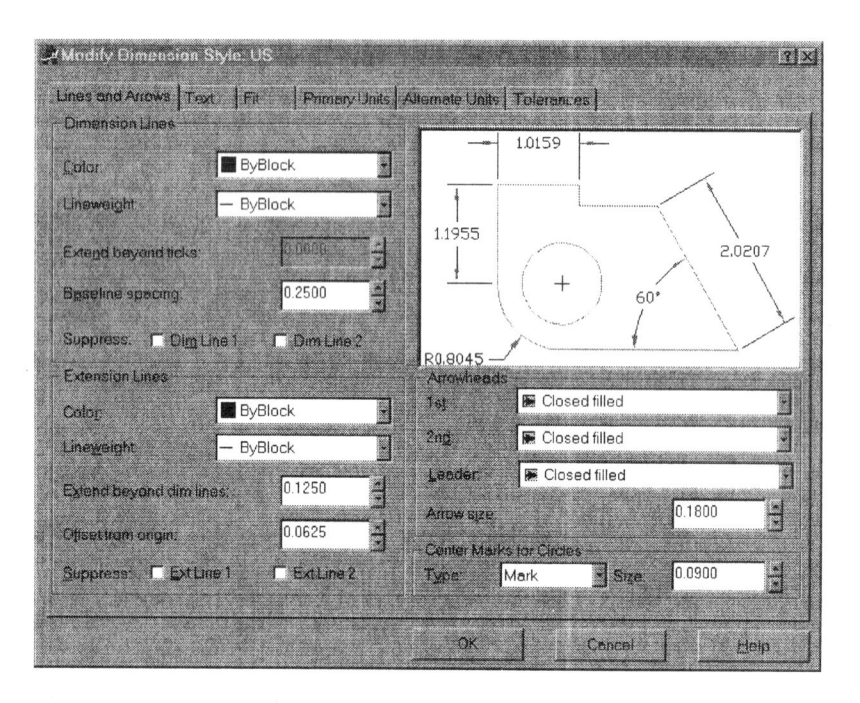

Figure 13.2 *The Lines and Arrows tab settings.*

5. Select the Text tab. Ensure that the settings are the same as those found in figure 13.3.

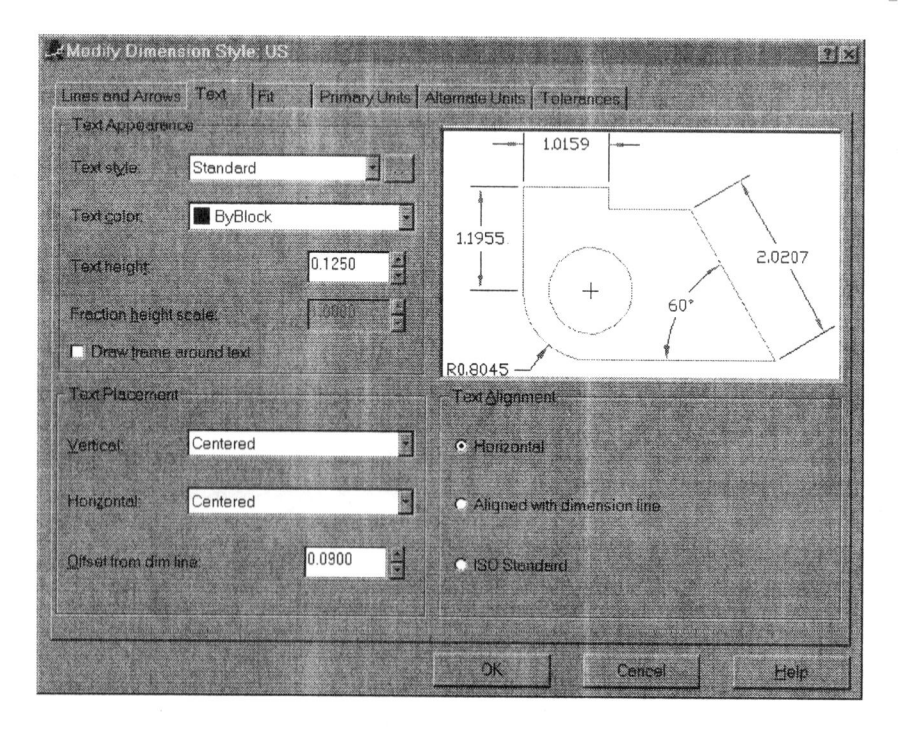

Figure 13.3 *The Text tab settings.*

6. No changes are needed in the Fit tab, so select the Primary Units tab next. Ensure that the settings are the same as those found in figure 13.4.

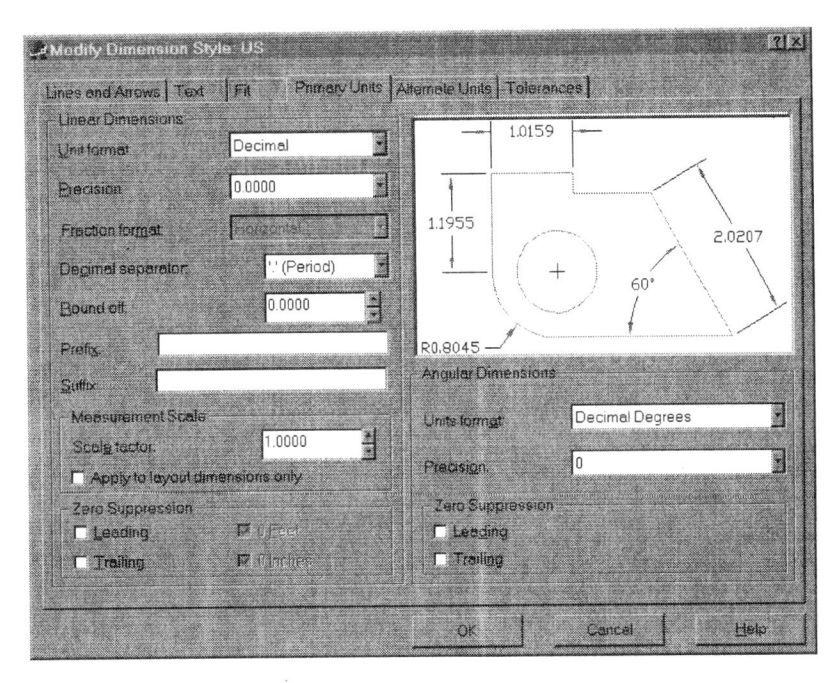

Figure 13.4 *The Primary Units tab settings.*

7. After making the necessary changes in the Primary Units tab, select OK. Your Dimension Style Manager dialog box should look like figure 13.5.

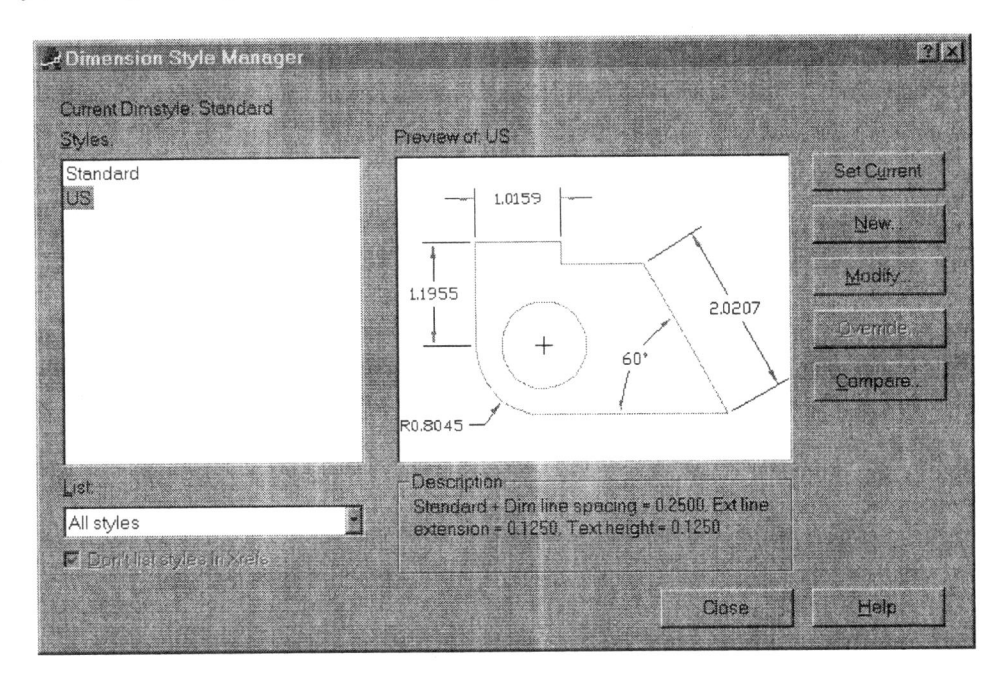

Figure 13.5 *The SI symbol.*

International System of Units (SI)

The SI system utilizes the millimeter (mm) as the common unit of measure. As a matter of fact, the ASME Y14.5M-1994 standard selects the millimeter as the default unit as denoted by the M following the standard number. This should be the standard chosen for all electronic drawings. To ensure that it is defined as to which system is being used, all drawings utilizing the SI system will include the SI symbol. The SI symbol not only informs the reader that the drawing utilizes the SI system of measurement, but it also describes which angle of projection is being utilized, first or third. Both the first angle (international) and third angle (United States) projection symbols are shown in figure 13.6.

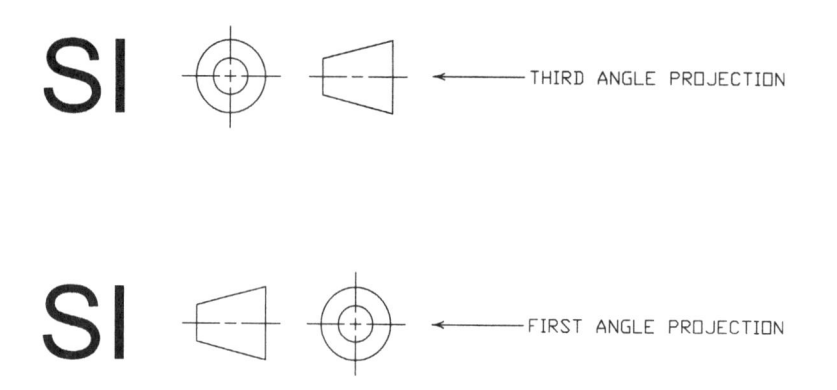

Figure 13.6 *First angle and third angle projection symbols.*

FOR THE PROFESSIONAL

This text does not describe in detail the difference between first and third angle projection. You should consult an Engineering Drawing book for more information concerning both of these theories. It may be necessary for you to create a first angle projection drawing in the future.

To create a dimension style that conforms to the SI system, folow figure 13.7 to 13.10. Begin by basing it on the US style created earlier.

SKILL BUILDER

Consider creating a prototype file that contains both of these dimension styles. You can combine these styles with the layers, linetypes, and user settings of other prototype files. You will then have a file that automates almost all of the mundane settings that are generally necessary for creating a new electronic drawing.

While dimension styles assist in creating the majority of electronic dimensions, they cannot be used in all instances. This is where the DDMODIFY command comes into play. Use this command to make slight modifications of dimensions that do not conform to the dimension style standards that have been established. Likewise, grips provide an excellent means of modifying locations of text, distances from other lines, and gaps between extension and object lines.

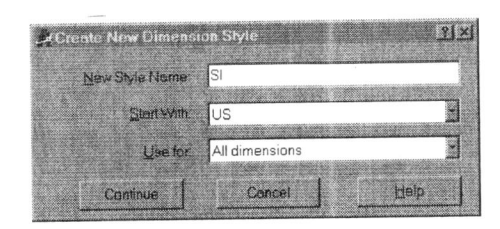

Figure 13.7 *Creating a new dimension style starting with the US style.*

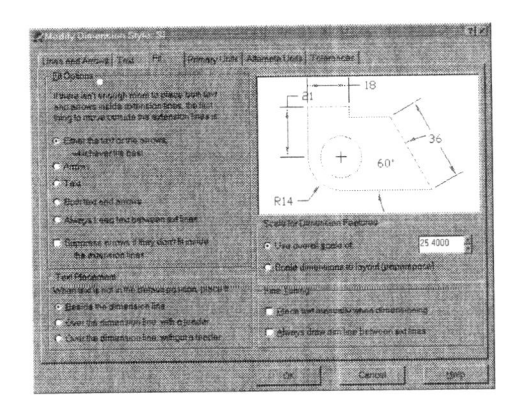

Figure 13.8 *Adjusting the overall scale in the Fit tab.*

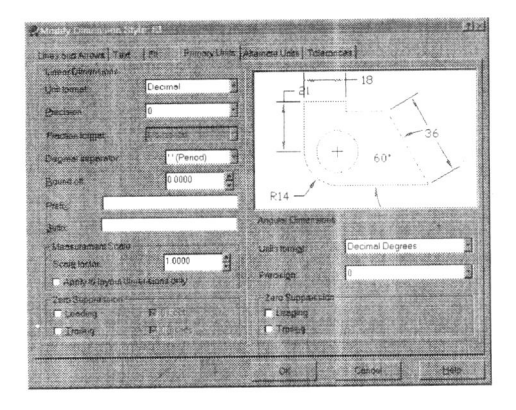

Figure 13.9 *Adjusting the precision in the Primary Units tab.*

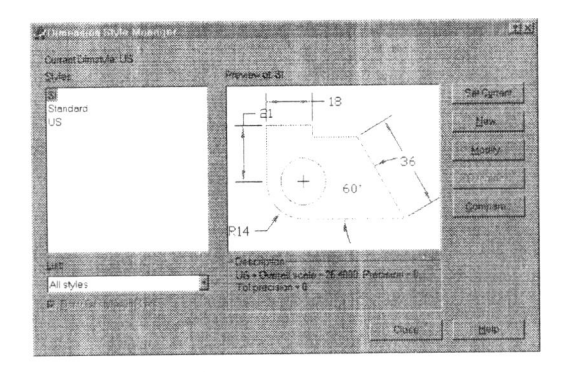

Figure 13.10 *The Dimension Style Manager dialog box with the SI and US dimension styles.*

Section 2: Linear and Radial Dimensioning

Both linear and radial dimensions were described in detail in figure 13.1. A discussion of their use, however, was very limited. This section will briefly address situations where each type of dimension would be used on an electronics drawing. If a concept or command is unfamiliar, you should consult the main text for more information so that each of these examples is understood.

Linear Dimensions

Linear dimensions are used to measure distances along the horizontal or vertical axis. The majority of all electronic dimensions will be linear. Look though the drawings presented in this workbook and in figure 13.1. Notice that almost all dimensions are horizontal and vertical.

Aligned Dimensions

Aligned dimensions are any dimensions that are not vertical or horizontal. Aligned dimensions are very useful when auxiliary views need to be dimensioned.

Radial Dimensioning

To create radial dimensions use the Radius and Diameter buttons located on the Dimension toolbar. While the Radius button is great for dimensioning the radius of arcs, dimensions created with the Dimension button do not conform to normal ASME standards. To dimension diameters, use the LEADER command and be sure to include the string "%%c" at the beginning of the text so that the diameter symbol (ø) will be included. An example of a proper diameter dimension using the LEADER command is shown in figure 13.1.

FOR THE PROFESSIONAL

For precision drawing, Geometric Dimensioning and Tolerancing (GD&T) is often used. Since GD&T is not common it is only occasionally used in electronic drafting. To create feature control frames, use the TOLERANCE command. See the AutoCAD manual for more information on this command.

Name _____

Unit 13 Review

1. The _____ command automates the creation of feature control frames.

2. The _____ system uses millimeters as the common unit of measure.

3. The _____ system uses inches as the common unit of measure.

4. ASME stands for _____ _____ _____ _____.

5. ANSI stands for _____ _____ _____ _____.

6. The current ASME standard for dimensioning and tolerancing is ASME _____ - _____.

7. The _____ _____ is included on all drawings that use millimeters as the common unit of measure.

8. True or False. The LEADER command provides an option for creating a feature control frame.

9. True or False. The LEADER command may be used to create a diameter dimension.

10. True or False. Once a dimension is created, it cannot be modified.

Unit 13 Assignment # 1

In this assignment you will create the Circuit Board Mount drawing shown in figure 13.11.

Follow the directions below to assist in the dimensioning of this drawing.

1. Create a new drawing named *Circuit Board Mount*.

2. Setup a drawing for an A-size sheet of paper using English units.

3. Set SNAP and GRID to your preferences.

4. Add a .9mm thick border around the drawing.

5. Re-create the views as shown on the following page.

6. Completely dimension the drawing as shown.

7. Ensure that layers, linetypes, and colors are used.

8. Create a dimension style that utilizes the U.S. Customary system.

9. Save the drawing when it is completed.

10. Plot the drawing.

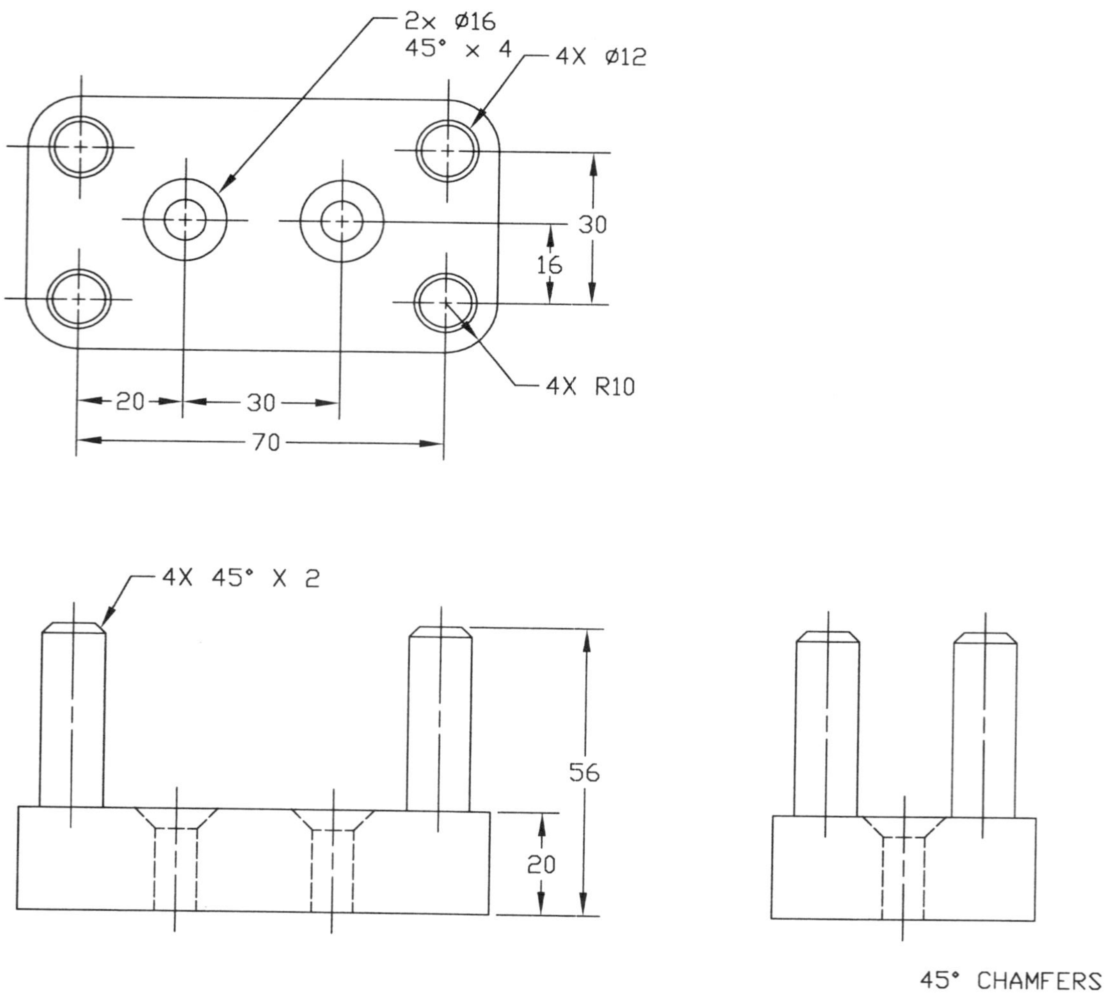

Figure 13.11 *The Circuit Board Mount drawing.*

Unit 13 Assignment # 2

In this assignment you will create the detail drawings that are a part of the C-Clamp working drawing as shown in figure 13.12.

1. Create a new drawing named *C-Clamp*.

2. Setup a drawing for an A-size sheet of paper using metric units.

3. Set SNAP and GRID to your preferences.

4. Add a .9mm thick border around the drawing.

5. Re-create the views as shown on the following page.

6. Completely dimension the views.

7. Create the SI symbol.

8. Add your name to the drawing. Do not add a title block. This drawing will be used again in Unit 16.

9. Plot the drawing at full scale.

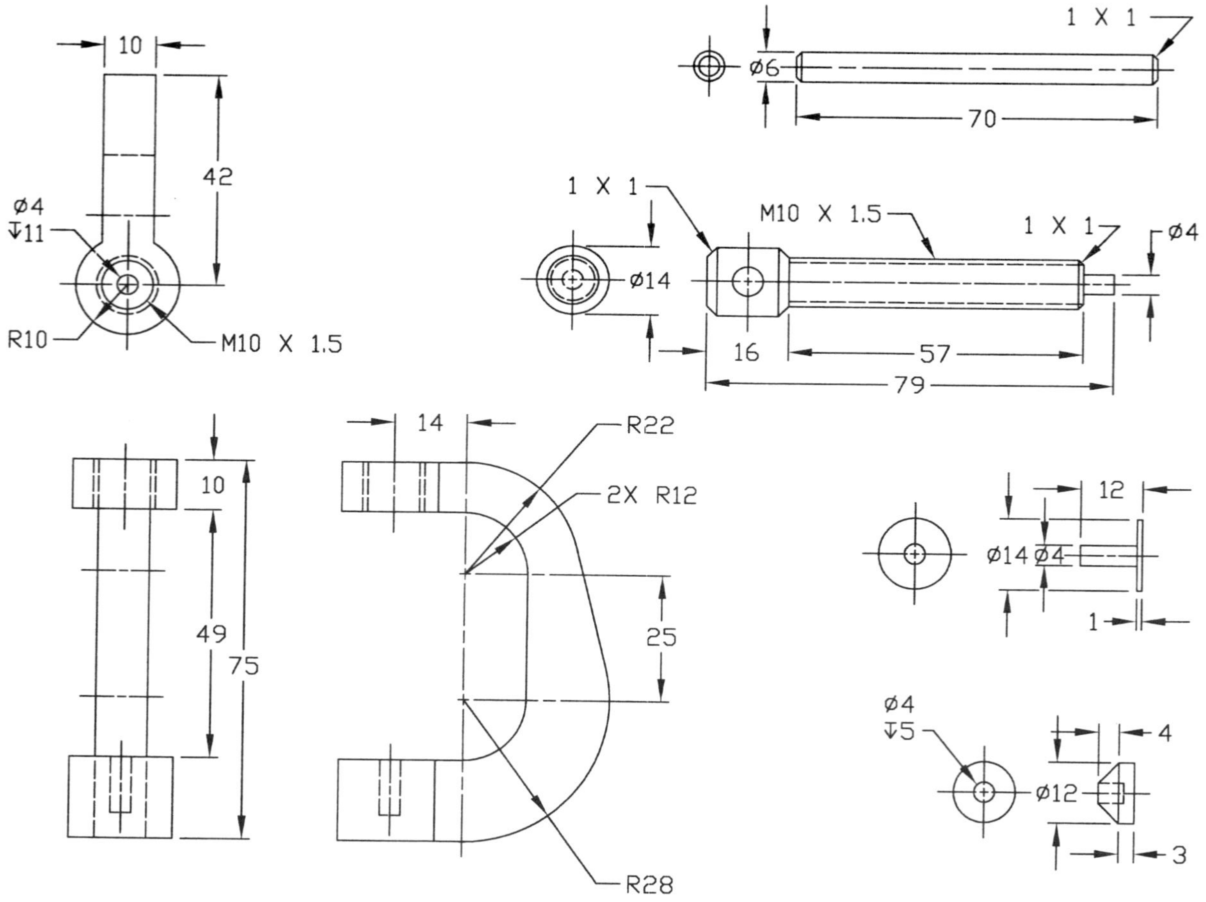

Figure 13.12 *The C-Clamp working drawing.*

Unit 14: Modifying Object Characteristics and Extracting Information from your Drawing

Overview

Each time you create an object, AutoCAD stores a great deal of information on it in a database. By accessing this database, you can change many characteristics of the object. You can also extract information from the database on the entire drawing, or on specific parts of the drawing.

Objectives

- Change the layer and linetype of objects on a electrical drawing
- Modify a polyline with PEDIT

Introduction

Editing geometry is a common task when creating drawings. In Unit 10, Basic Editing Skills, you worked with several editing commands such as MOVE, TRIM, EXTEND, FILLET, and CHAMFER. In addition to these commands, you can also directly access the database for a specific object and modify its characteristics. Polylines are an important part of electronics drafting. When circuit boards contain sharp corners, problems can be encountered during manufacturing. The PEDIT command can be used to round off the corners of an existing polyline.

Section 1: Modifying Object Properties

By accessing the database for selected objects, you can easily change many of their characteristics. By using the Properties dialog box (figure 14.1), you can move several selected objects to a different layer. You can also change other object properties, such as color, linetype, linetype scale, and thickness. The Properties dialog box can be accessed as follows:

- Select the Properties button from the Object Properties toolbar.

- Select Properties from the Modify pulldown menu.

- Type **properties** at the Command: prompt.

You can also edit specific information stored in the AutoCAD database for individual objects. The information that appears in the Properties dialog box depends on the type of object selected as shown in figure 14.2.

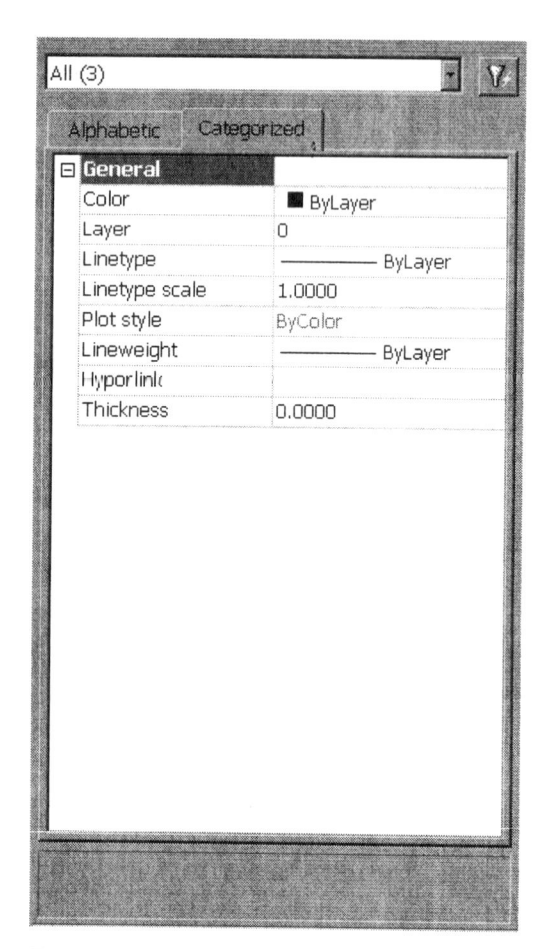

Figure 14.1 *The Properties dialog box can be used to modify object characteristics of multiple objects.*

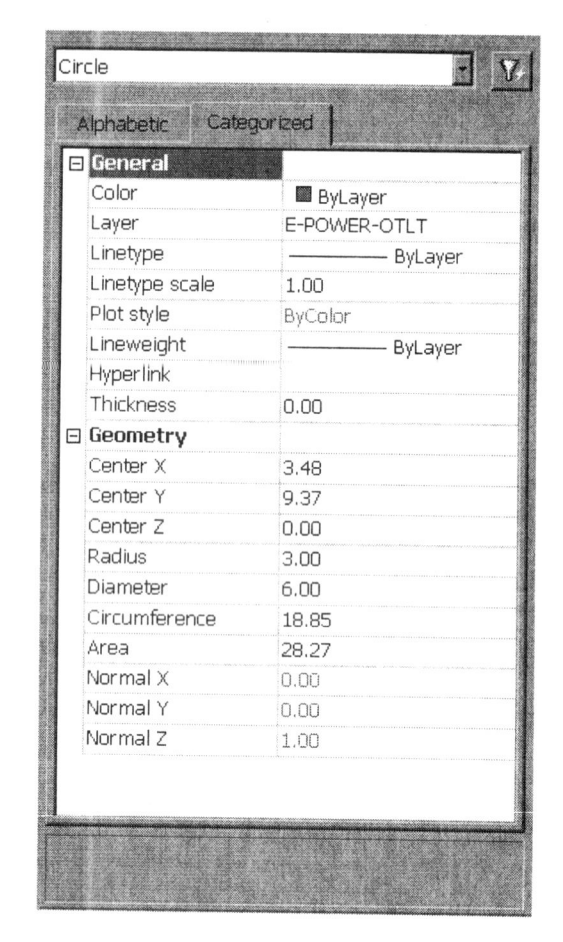

Figure 14.2 *When selecting single objects the information displayed in the Properties dialog box depends upon the object selected.*

Moving an Object to a Different Layer

In Unit 6, Creating Basic Geometry, and Unit 12, Advanced Drawing Techniques, you were working with a resistor symbol. Many electrical drawings will contain more than one resistor symbol, depending upon the type of circuit. Resistor symbols found on electrical drawings include common, adjustable, and tapped. Since the resistor symbols are similar, you can easily copy one symbol, make the necessary changes, and move it to a new layer. Figure 14.3 shows general and adjustable resistor symbols.

To create the adjustable resistor symbol, first copy the general symbol. In the copied symbol, add the arrow. Creating a dimensioning leader can do this. Create a new layer called RES-A, color 171. To move the new symbol to the correct layer, access the Change Properties dialog box. At the `Select Objects:` prompt, select *all* of the lines that comprise the adjustable resistor symbol. When the Change Properties dialog box appears, select the <u>L</u>ayer button to access the Select Layer dialog box. Choose the RES-A layer. In one simple step, the adjustable resistor symbol is changed to a new layer.

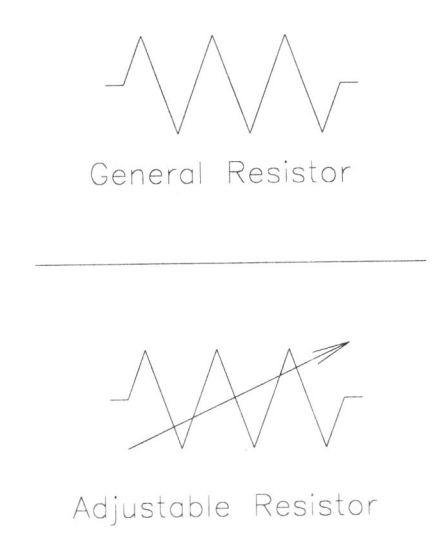

Figure 14.3 *General and adjustable resistor symbols.*

Section 2: Editing a Polyline with PEDIT

The polyline command has a lot of applications in electrical drafting. As mentioned in Unit 12, Advanced Drawing Techniques, polylines have several special features that make them very useful when creating printed circuit boards. Creating circuit boards with 90° corners can create etching problems during the manufacturing process. Figure 14.4 shows a typical circuit. The one on the right was created using 90-degree corners, which is incorrect. Angling corners created the one on the left, which is the preferred method. This figure is displayed with FILL set to OFF. When creating the circuit board, you can use the ARC option of polyline, but in most cases it is easier to create the wiring trace as a series of straight polylines. If the polyline is too straight, it can be changed to include more curves using the PEDIT command.

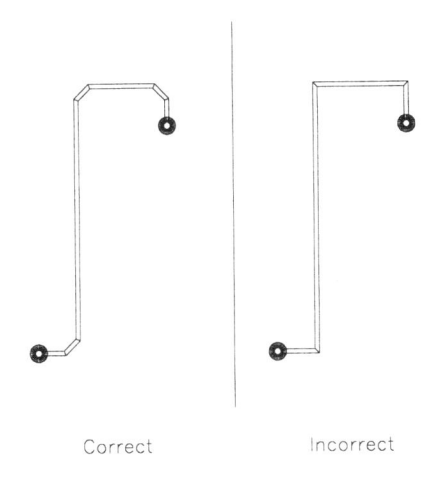

Figure 14.4 *Circuit boards created with 90-degree corners can create problems during manufacturing.*

Using PEDIT to Create a Spline Curve

The original polyline can be edited at any time to generate fit or spline curves shown in figure 14.5. Editing a polyline into a spline curve eliminates sharp edges or corners. The two types of spline curves that can be created from an existing polyline are Quadratic and Cubic. By editing the existing polyline and changing it into a spline curve, all sharp edges are removed and a smooth curve results. The type of curve used doesn't matter. Select the type of curve that works best in a given situation.

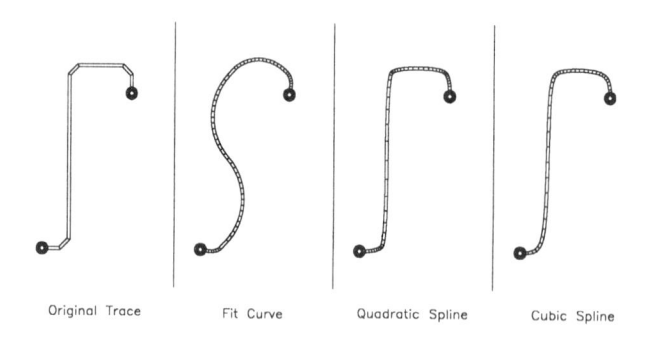

Figure 14.5 *Different curves available from the PEDIT command.*

The SPLINETYPE system variable determines the type of spline curve that is created. The default value of 6 generates a cubic spline. If you set SPLINETYPE to 5, a quadratic spline is generated. SPLINETYPE only accepts these two values, 5 or 6. The variable must be set *before* creating the spline.

The SPLINESEGS system variable controls the number of line segments created when the spline PEDIT option is used. The default value is 8, with a maximum value of 20. Increasing the SPLINESEGS variable increases the quality of the resultant spline, but also slows down AutoCAD and increases the size of the drawing file. Figure 14.6 shows two quadratic splines (SPLINETYPE set to 5). One was created with SPLINESEGS set to 8, and the other with SPLINESEGS set to 20.

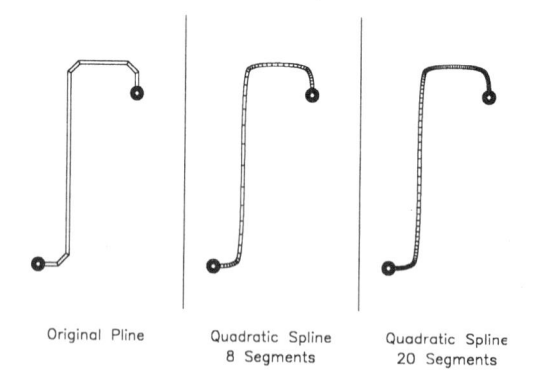

Figure 14.6 *The effect of changing the SPLINESEGS system variable on a quadratic spline.*

If the resulting curve or spline is not what you wanted, the PEDIT command Decurve will remove all curves from a polyline.

Name _____

Unit 14 Review

1. When generating a spline curve from an existing polyline, the vertices used as the curve's control points come from _____.

2. The two types of spline curves that can be created are _____ and _____.

3. Increasing the value of the SPLINESEGS variable _____ the number of segments in the resulting spline curve.

4. The _____ system variable governs the type of spline curve created.

5. When creating a wiring diagram, you should avoid making _____ types of corners.

6. To display the original polyline on screen after creating a spline, change the _____ system variable.

7. The _____ command determines whether polylines and donuts are displayed filled in or segmented.

8. You should maintain enough free disk space on your storage device that is _____ the size of the drawing.

9. To rename objects such as layers, linetypes, or text styles in a dialog box, use the _____ dialog box.

10. To change a polyline into a series of normal lines and arcs, use the _____ command.

Unit 14 Assignment #1

1. Begin a new drawing named POWERSUP, using the SCHEMATIC template drawing created in previous units.

2. Draw the Power Supply shown in figure 14.7, using the symbols available on the drawing. Creation of the diode symbol was discussed in Unit 12, Advanced Drawing Techniques.

3. Create your own symbols for the switch, testing links, LED, and adjustable resistor.

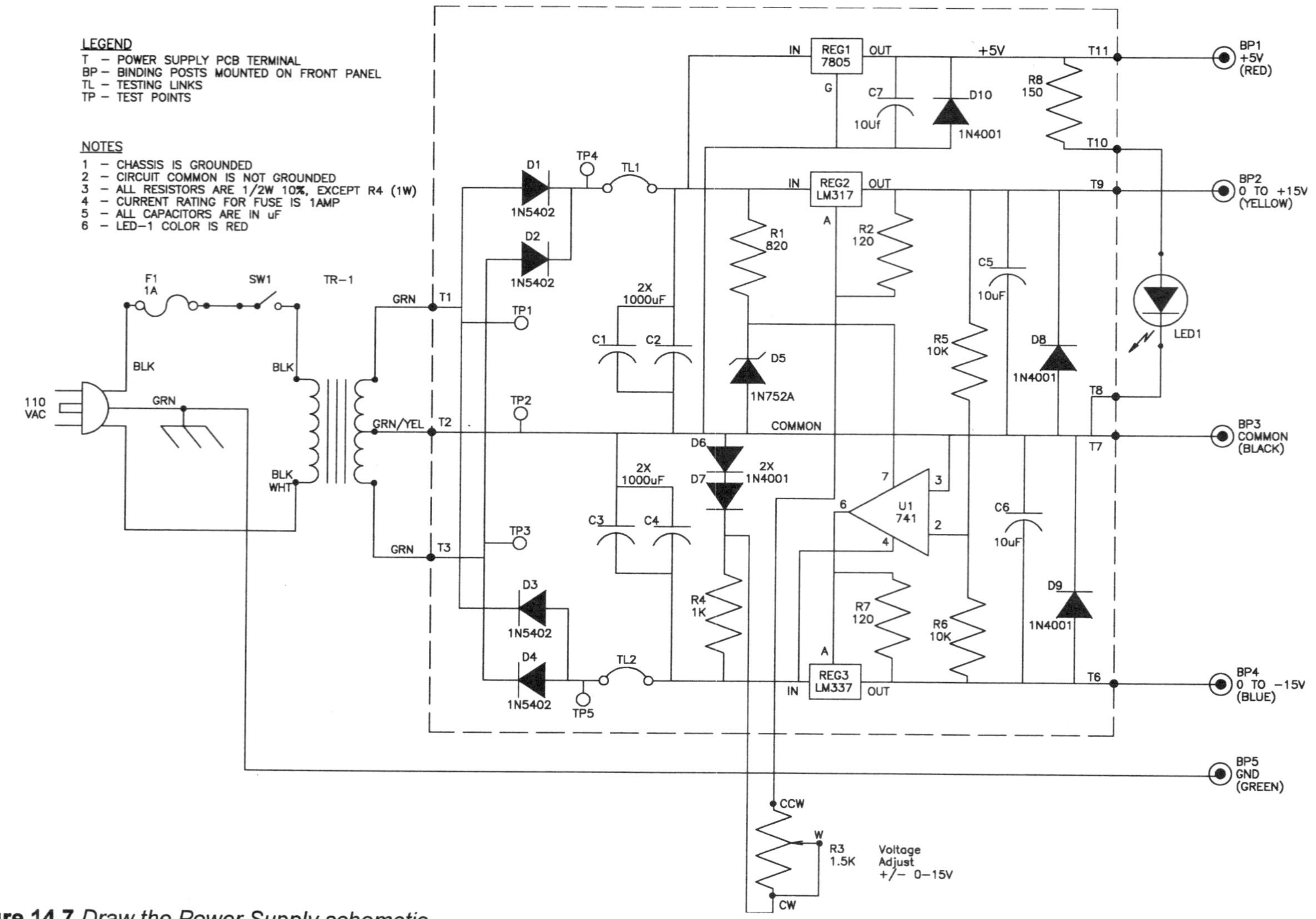

Figure 14.7 *Draw the Power Supply schematic.*

Unit 15: Using Symbols and Attributes

Overview

Many electronics drawings use the same geometry over and over. The resistor symbol, commonly found on printed circuit board drawings, is one example. AutoCAD allows you create an object such as the resistor symbol and import it into other drawings. You can also attach information to a symbol, such as the manufacturer and price of a specific object.

Objectives

- Create a resistor symbol for use in a printed circuit board drawing.
- Insert the resistor symbol into a drawing.
- Attach information to a resistor symbol with attributes.

Introduction

The ability to use common geometry over and over is another big advantage to using a CAD system over manual drafting. If you manage your files and drawings properly, you should *never* have to draw an object more than once. Another advantage of AutoCAD over manual drafting is the ability to attach information to an object. You also have the option of displaying this information on the screen or plot, or having it remain hidden. You can also extract this information into a spreadsheet or database.

Section 1: Creating and Inserting a Block of the Resistor Symbol

Blocks, which can be used to represent symbols, are created like any other object using your standard drawing and editing symbols. A block is defined as a single object, composed of many other objects. You can also block objects from other drawings and insert them into the current drawing. If you know the geometry you are creating will be used again, create a block of it. File management is a very important concept when dealing with blocks. When you create a block, you must give it a name and store it in a location easily found later.

Creating a Block of a Resistor Symbol

Many printed circuit board drawings contain the standard resistor symbol shown in figure 15.1. The resistor symbol is a good candidate for a block, since it is used repeatedly. To create a block of the symbol, you first need to draw the symbol. Creating this symbol was discussed in Unit 12, Advanced Drawing Techniques. If you have a symbol that was created in a previous drawing, you can access that drawing and block the symbol directly from the drawing. You do not have to redraw something to create a block of it if it has already been created.

The first step in creating a block of the resistor symbol is to determine the insertion point. A good location would be the left end of the polyline shown in figure 15.2. This insertion point is used when the block is inserted into a drawing. The block appears on the screen with the screen crosshairs at the insertion point.

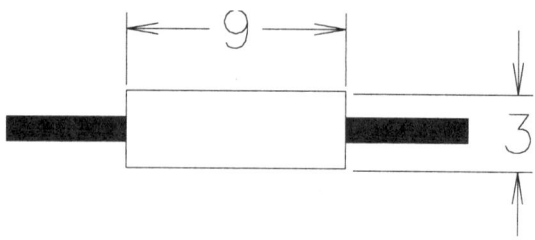

Figure 15.1 *The resistor symbol, commonly found on a printed circuit board.*

Figure 15.2 *Selecting an insertion point for the resistor symbol.*

After creating or finding the symbol on another drawing and determining the insertion point, use the WBLOCK command. This will create a separate drawing file of the objects you define as part of the block. You can access the WBLOCK command by:

- Typing **wblock** at the Command: prompt.

After invoking the WBLOCK command, the Write Block dialog box appears. It is very important that you select the correct drive and subdirectory where you want to store the block. You also need to name the block. Don't include a file extension since AutoCAD automatically adds one. The Write Block dialog box is shown in figure 15.3.

After entering the file name and selecting the correct drive and path, you need to determine the insertion base point. At this point you can enter the coordinates, or select the Pick point button. Selecting the Pick point button will return you to the drawing editor where you can select the end of the resistor using ENDpoint object snap.

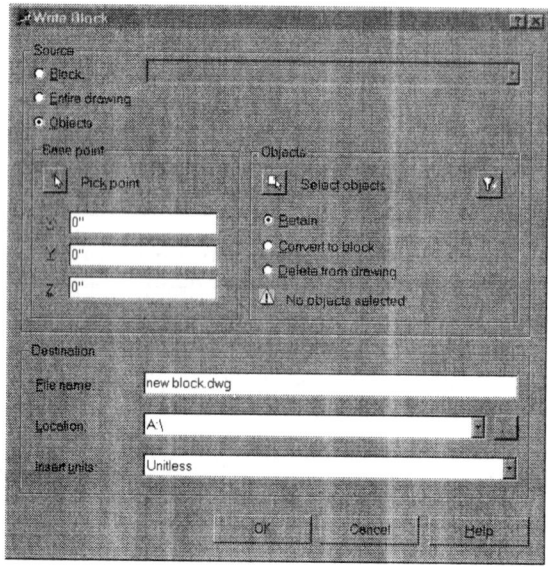

Figure 15.3 *The Write Block dialog box.*

After selecting the insertion base point, you need to select the object that will comprise the block. Choose the Select Objects button to return to the drawing editor where you can use any object selection method (such as window, fence, crossing window) to pick all of the objects that make up the door symbol.

Inserting the Resistor Symbol into a Drawing

After creating a block of the resistor symbol, you can insert it into a drawing. When you insert the resistor symbol into a drawing, you must specify four things:

- The name, drive, and path of the resistor block.

- The point where you want the resistor block inserted.

- The rotation of the resistor symbol. This will depend upon the orientation of the objects on which the symbol is being inserted.

- The resistor block scale in the X-, Y-, and Z-axis. All symbols should be drawn full scale, and inserted into the drawing at a 1=1 scale.

To insert the resistor into the current drawing, use the Insert dialog box shown in figure 15.4. You can access this dialog box as follows:

- Select the Insert Block button on the Draw or Insert toolbar.

- Type **insert** at the Command: prompt.

- Select Block from the Insert pull down menu.

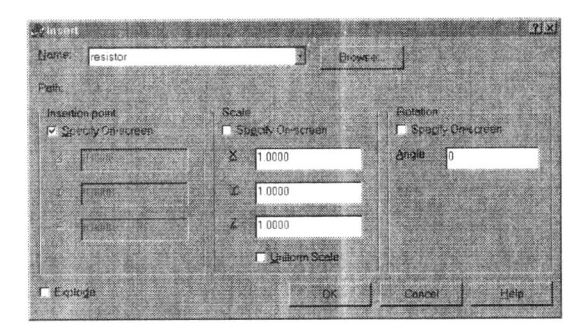

Figure 15.4 *The Insert dialog box, used to insert the resistor symbol into the current drawing.*

To insert the resistor symbol into the current drawing, select the Browse... button in the Insert dialog box. This accesses the Select Drawing File dialog box as shown in figure 15.4. Change to the correct drive and directory and choose the resistor symbol file.

When you are returned to the Insert dialog box, you have the option of entering the insertion point, scale, and rotation of the resistor block in the dialog box or at the Command: prompt. By default, the Specify Parameters on Screen box is checked, which will return you to the Command: prompt. If you know the insertion point, scale, and rotation, you can enter this information directly in the Insert dialog box.

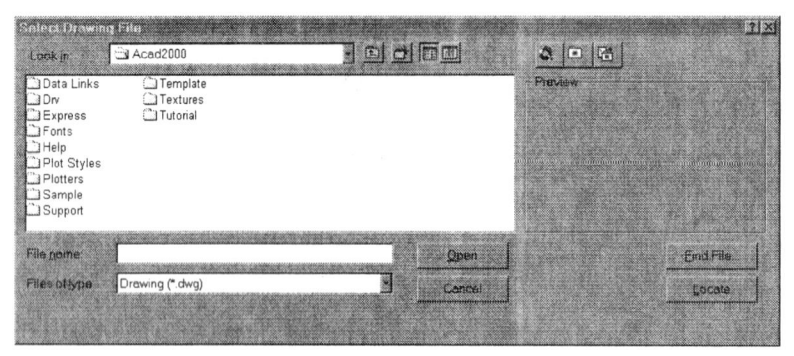

Figure 15.5 *The Select Drawing File dialog box, used to select the resistor block.*

If you leave the Specify Parameters on Screen box checked, you are returned to the drawing editor and prompted for the `Specify insertion point or [Scale/X/Y/Z/Rotate/ PScale/PX/PY/PZ/PRotate]:`. The insertion point for the door symbol is the end of the resistor, which was specified when the block was originally defined. As you move the crosshairs, AutoCAD dynamically moves the resistor symbol on the screen. You can select the insertion point on screen, or type in the absolute coordinates where you want the resistor block inserted.

You can change the `Scale` factor for the symbol by entering an **S** at the prompt. Enter the scale factor of the resistor symbol. Remember, the scale factor for the resistor symbol should be 1, which is the default. By entering X, Y, or Z you can enter different scale factors.

You can also `Rotate` the symbol by entering an **R**. Many times you will have to rotate the symbol to align with the other objects.

Section 2: Adding Information to a Resistor Symbol with Attributes

The procedure for creating a symbol with attached attributes is similar to the procedure used to create the resistor symbol. Creating an attribute to associate with a resistor involves the following steps:

1. Create the resistor symbol using your geometry creation and editing commands.

2. Define the attribute using the ATTDEF or DDATTDEF commands.

3. Use the BLOCK or WBLOCK commands to convert the resistor objects and attributes into a named block. When the Select objects: prompt appears, select all of the drawing objects and attributes.

4. Insert the resistor's symbol and associated attributes into the current drawing using the INSERT or DDINSERT commands.

Creating the Resistor Symbol

The first step is to create the resistor symbol shown in figure 15.1 just like you did when we created a WBLOCK. As before, if you already have a resistor symbol on another drawing, you can use it.

Defining the Resistor Attributes

To define an attribute for the resistor, first do the following:

- Type **ddattdef** at the Command: prompt.

This will access the Attribute Definition dialog box as shown in figure 15.6.

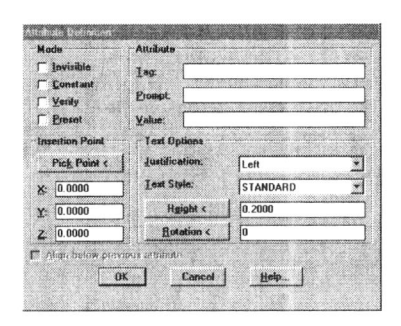

Figure 15.6 *The Attribute Definition dialog box, used to enter all attribute definitions for the resistor.*

For both attributes, use the Standard style, with a height of 1 mm. We will use the following values for the first resistor attribute:

    Mode: Invisible

    Tag: **POWER**

    Prompt: **Resistor power at 70 degrees F.**

    Value: **1/2 watt**

Use the following values for the second resistor attribute:

    Mode: Invisible

    Tag: **GRADE**

    Prompt: **Resistor grade**

    Value: **Industrial**

Check the Align below previous attribute box.

At this point the drawing looks like figure 15.7, with the resistor and two defined attributes.

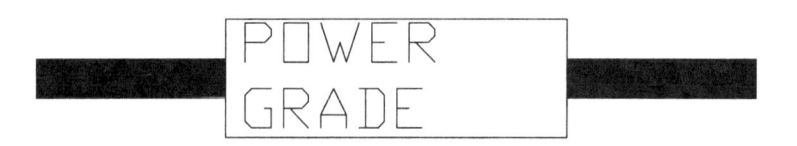

Figure 15.7 *The resistor with two defined attributes.*

Creating a Block of the Resistor and Attributes

When creating a block of the resistor and attributes, use the same procedure described for making a block of the resistor symbol. When adding attributes to a block, however, first select the attributes *individually*. This will ensure you are prompted for the attributes in the correct order. After selecting the attributes, select the objects that make up the resistor.

Inserting the Block of the Resistor and Attributes

When inserting the resistor and attributes block, use the same procedure that was used when the resistor symbol was inserted in the previous section. The only difference is you will be prompted for the power and grade of the resistor. This allows you to confirm the power and grade. If the ATTDIA system variable is set to 1, the prompt will be displayed in a dialog box. If ATTDIA is set to 0, you will be prompted for the values at the Command: prompt.

After inserting the resistor, the attributes will not appear on screen because both attributes were defined as invisible. To see the attributes, set the ATTDISP prompt to ON. All attributes are now visible as shown in figure 15.8.

Figure 15.8 *The inserted resistor symbol, with both attributes displayed.*

Name _____

Unit 15 Review

1. When creating geometry on a CAD system, you should never have to draw it more than _____.

2. Four commands that can be used to create the geometry for a BLOCK symbol are _____, _____, _____, and _____.

3. When a WBLOCK is written, it can be used _____ of the current drawing.

4. File management is important when creating a WBLOCK because: _____.

5. When creating a block symbol, it should always be drawn at _____ scale.

6. The insertion base point on a block is used to: _____.

7. Existing blocks can be renamed using the _____ command.

8. If you are inserting a drawing file for which you did not specify the base point, the _____ location becomes the insertion base point by default.

9. When a block is created from a group of objects, it is defined as a _____ object.

10. A text string that can be used to label or describe a block is called an _____.

Unit 15 Assignment #1

Open the PCB drawing you have been working on in the previous units. Create a WBLOCK of the symbols shown in figure 15.9. When blocking the symbols, use the file name displayed next to each symbol. Select the insertion point indicated by the arrow on each symbol.

1. Open the PCBPOWER drawing you created in Unit 7, Annotating a Drawing with Text and Hatching, as shown in figure 15.10.

2. Using the following table, insert the major components. Your drawing should look like figure 15.11.

Name	X Location	Y Location	Rotation
WECAPC3	50	167	0
WECAPC3	50	150	0
WECAPC3	35	125	180
WECAPC3	35	108	180
WREG3	107	160	0
WREG3	107	142	0
WREG3	107	124	0
WICU2	62	130	0

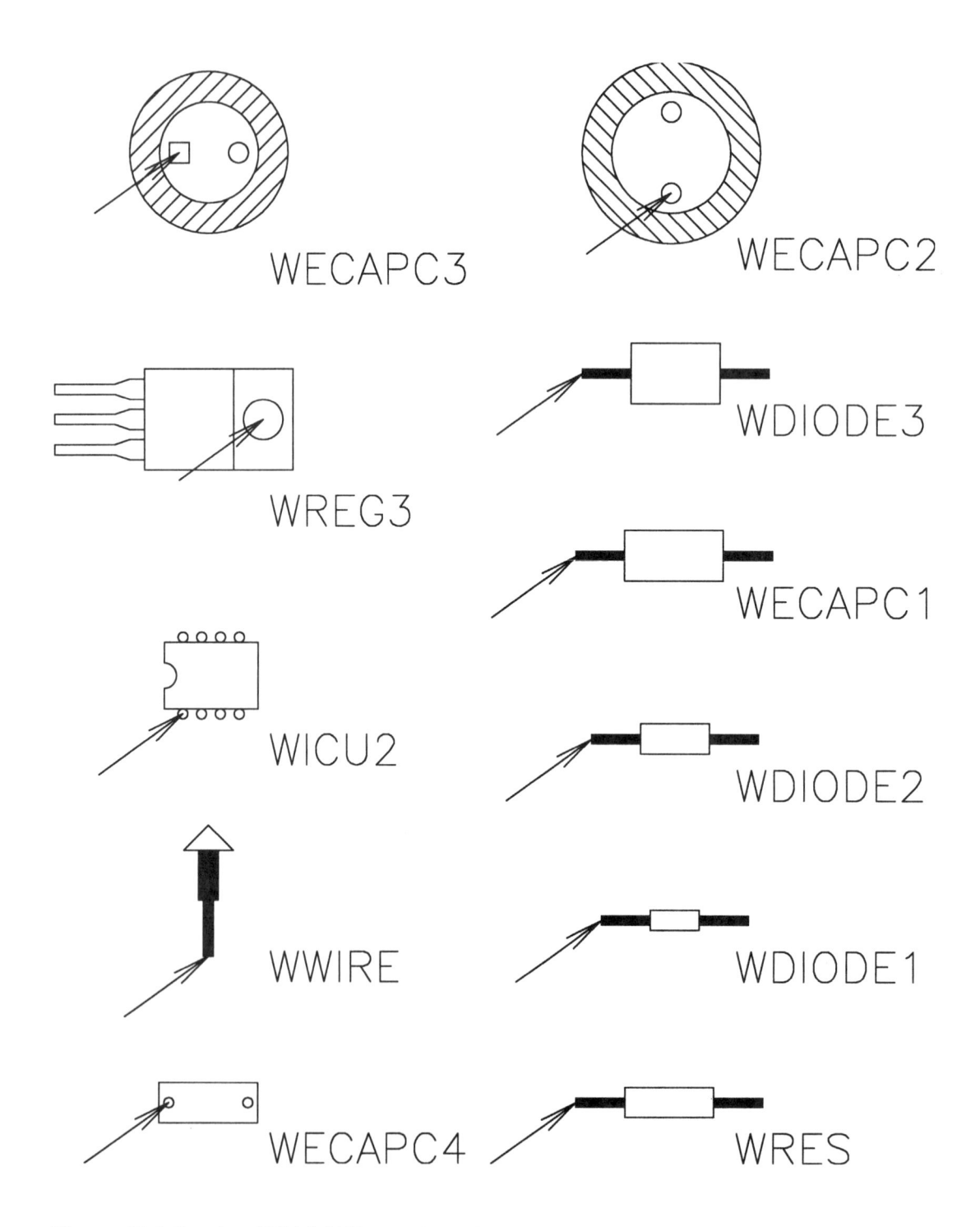

Figure 15.9 *Create a WBLOCK for each symbol.*

Figure 15.10 *The PCBPOWER drawing created in Unit 7.*

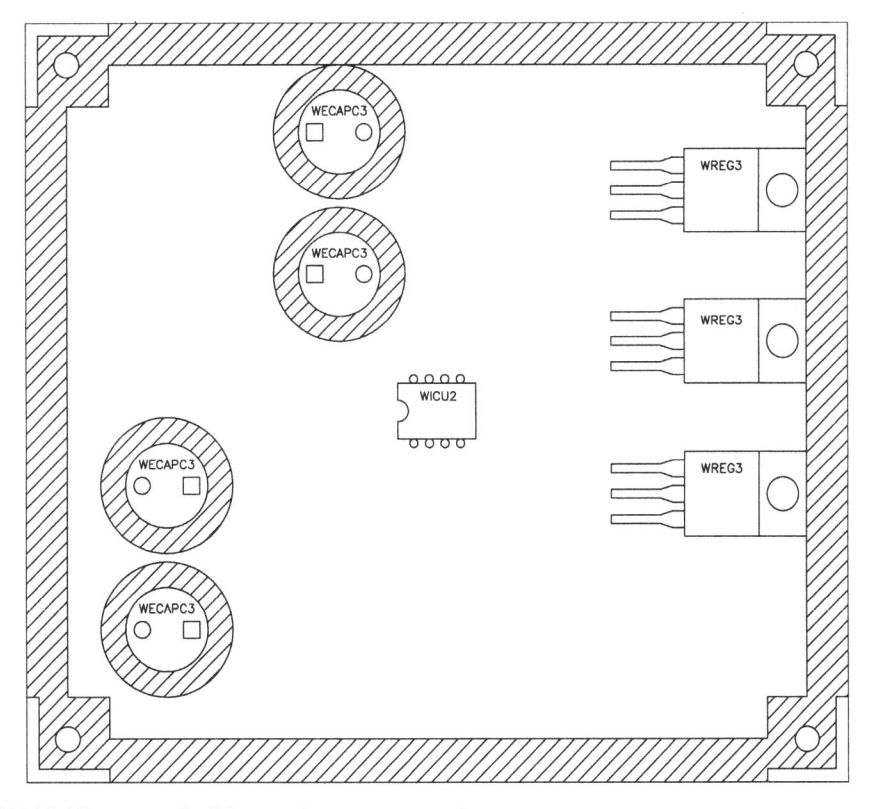

Figure 15.11 *Placement of the major components.*

3. Create a new layer called ICPAD, color 230. Using the following table, insert large IC pads. To create a large IC pad, use the DONUT command with a 1.5mm inside diameter and 4mm outside diameter.

X Location	Y Location
22	103
27	97
32	97
37	97
80	97
89	97
95	97
108	103
108	109
108	115

4. After inserting the IC pads, insert WWIRE symbols at the ends of the large IC pads. Your drawing should look like figure 15.12.

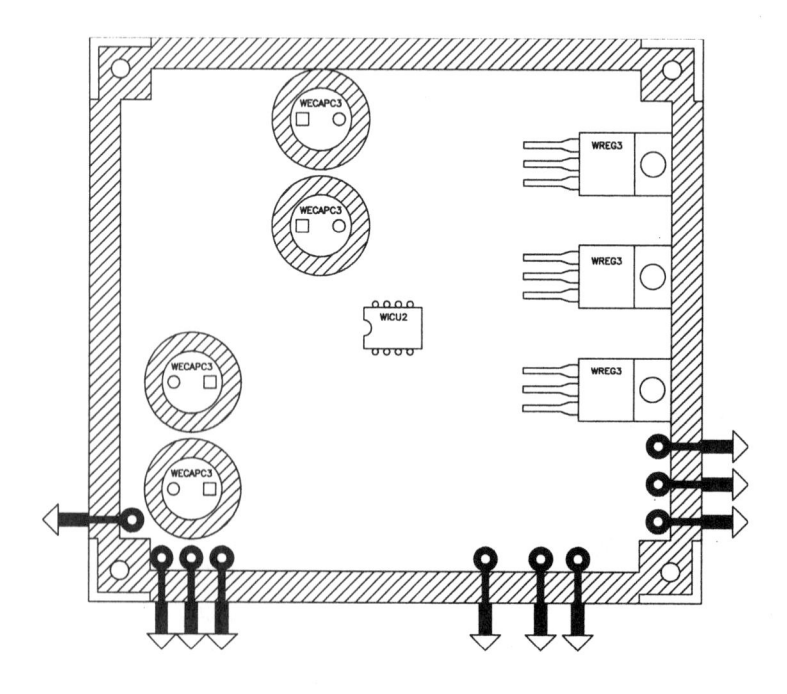

Figure 15.12 *Insertion of the large IC pads and the WWIRE symbols.*

5. Continue inserting the remainder of the major components as shown in figure 15.13.

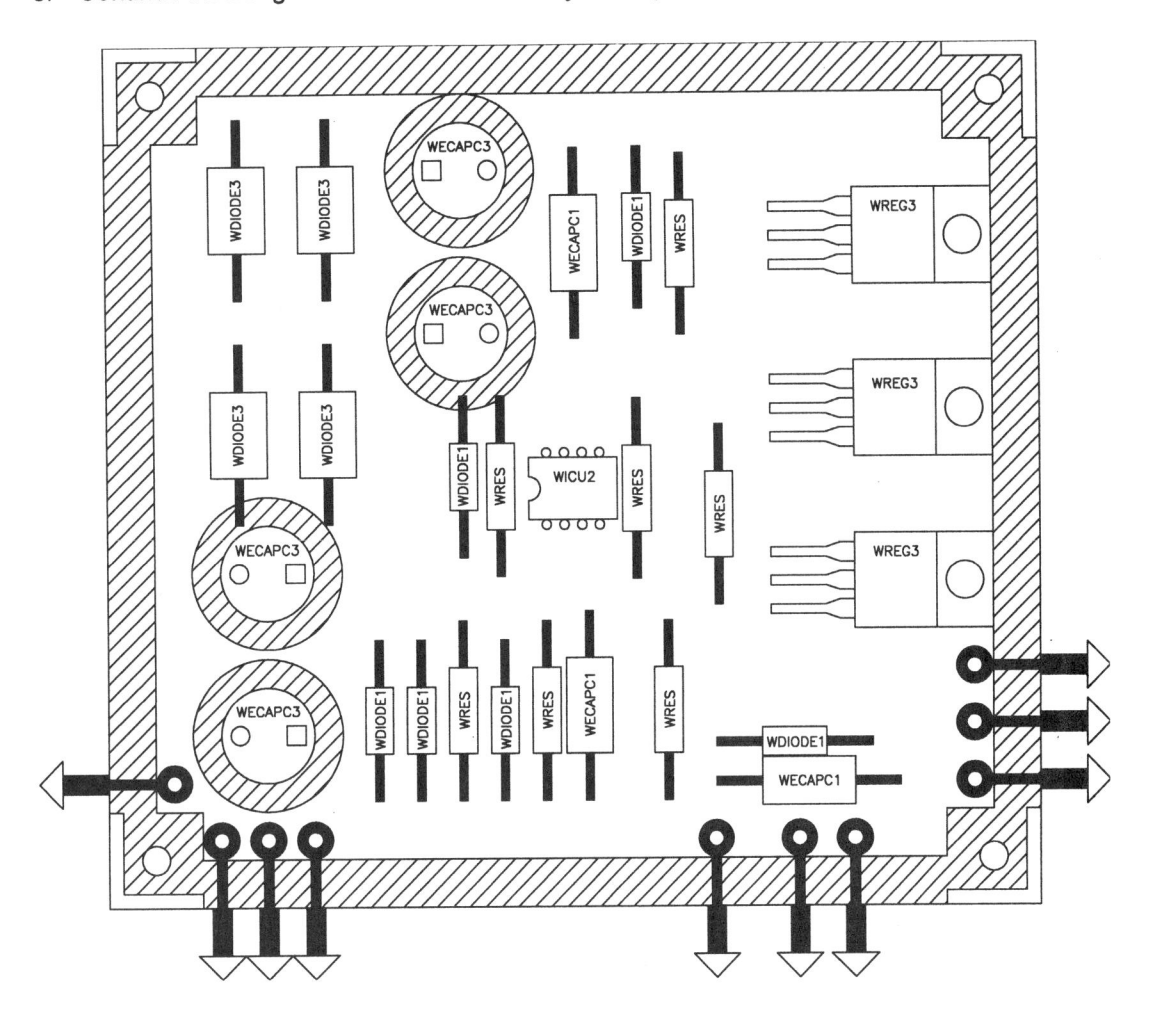

Figure 15.13 *Insertion locations of all major components.*

6. Create a new layer called ICPADS, color 222. Insert small IC pads on the connection points of the major components and other locations as shown in figure 15.14. To create a small IC pad, use the DONUT command with a 1mm inside diameter and 3mm outside diameter.

7. Add the remaining large IC pads and another WWIRE symbol as shown in figure 15.14. Create a new layer called ICPADICU, color 214. Create the ICU pads as shown in figure 15.15, using a PLINE with a width of .375. Begin by drawing a PLINE 1 mm long, followed by an arc, a line, and another arc. An alternative construction method would be to first create the figure using conventional lines and arcs. Issue the PEDIT command and join the sections, then change the width to .375. Copy the ICU pads onto the ICU itself, aligning the center of the ICU circle with the center of the ICU pad's arc. Figure 15.15 is shown with FILL set to OFF.

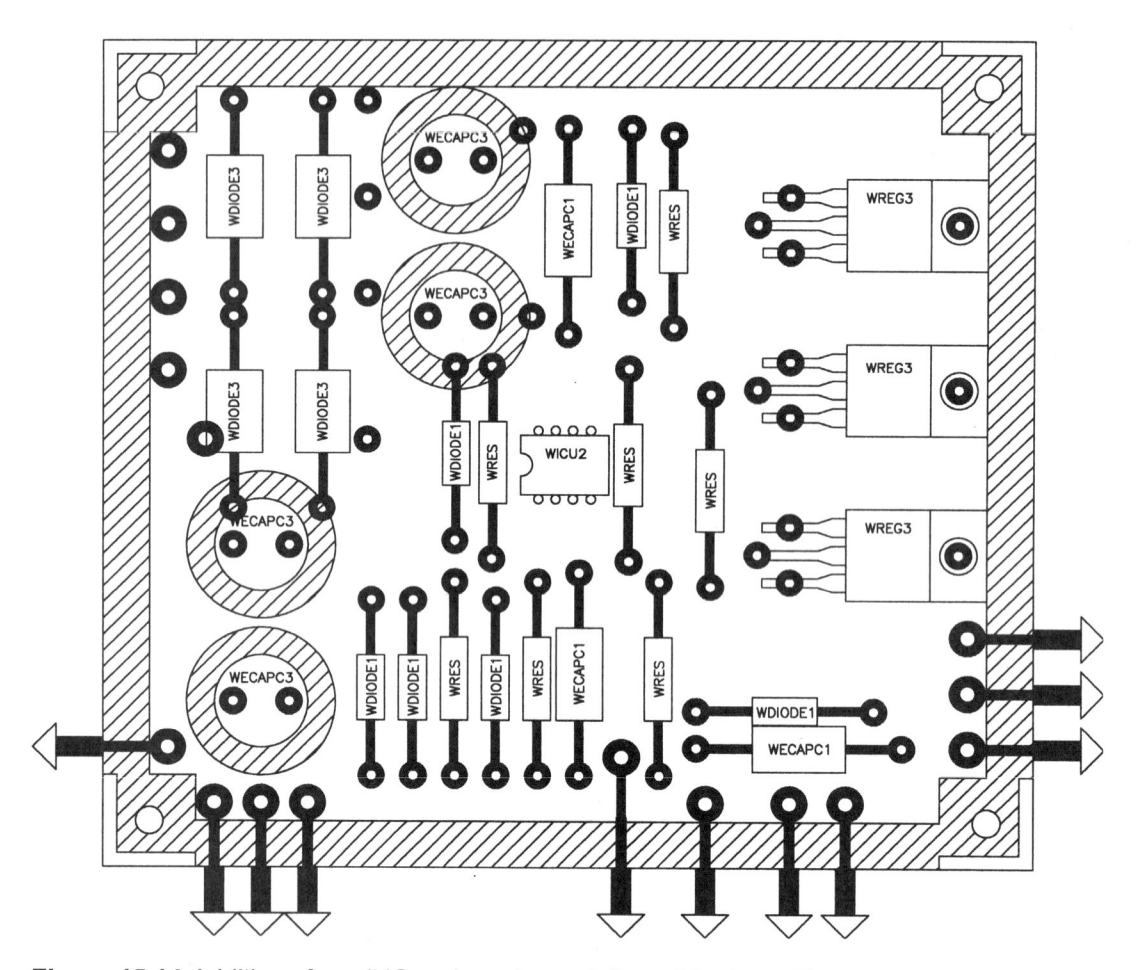

Figure 15.14 *Addition of small IC pads and completion of the large IC pads.*

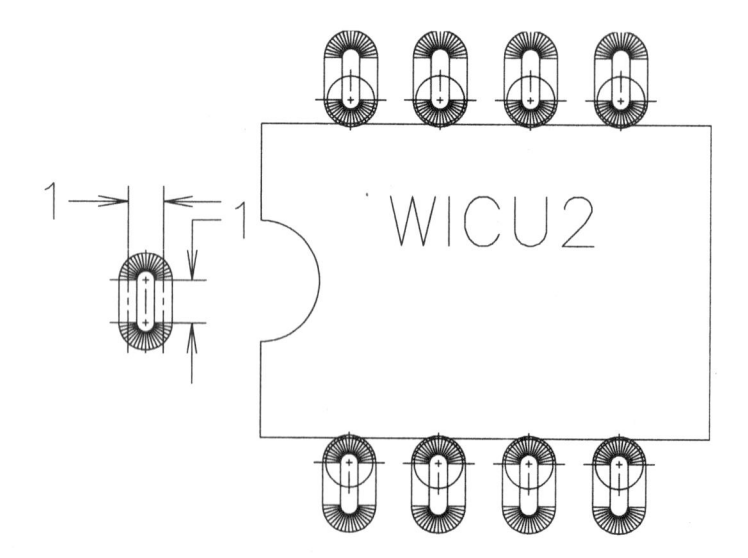

Figure 15.15 *Creating and copying the ICU pads.*

8. Use a PLINE width of 1.25 mm for the Common conductor and three regular conductors as shown in figure 15.16. Place them on a new layer called TRACE, color red. To make the drawing easier to see, turn off the WIRE layer. You may also want to turn off some or all of the components to make the drawing easier to work on.

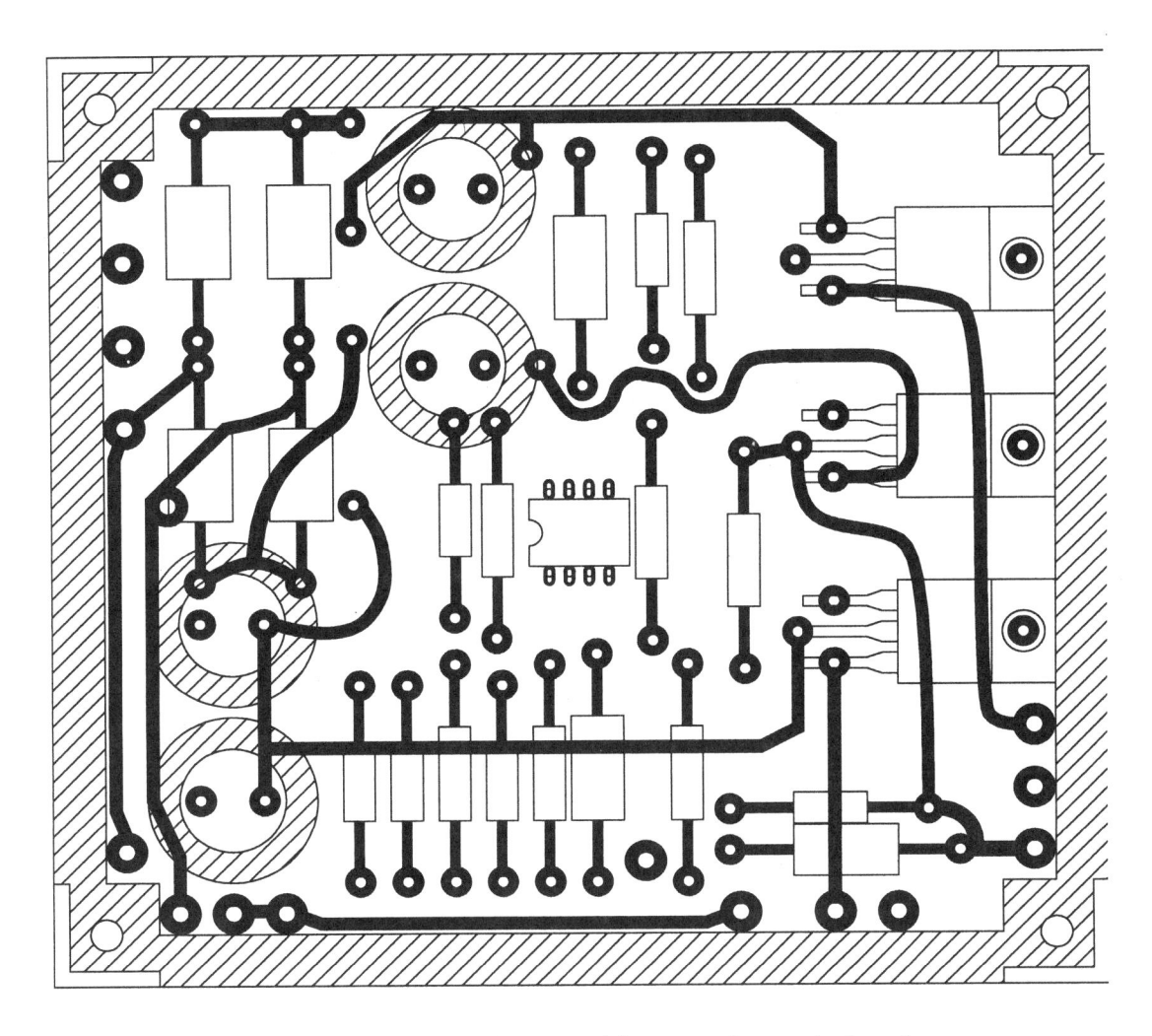

Figure 15.16 *Adding the Common conductor and three regular conductor wires.*

9. Use a PLINE width of .75 mm for the non-power conductors as shown in figure 15.17. Place these lines on a new layer called TRACES, color 54. Maintain a minimum distance of 1 mm between conductors.

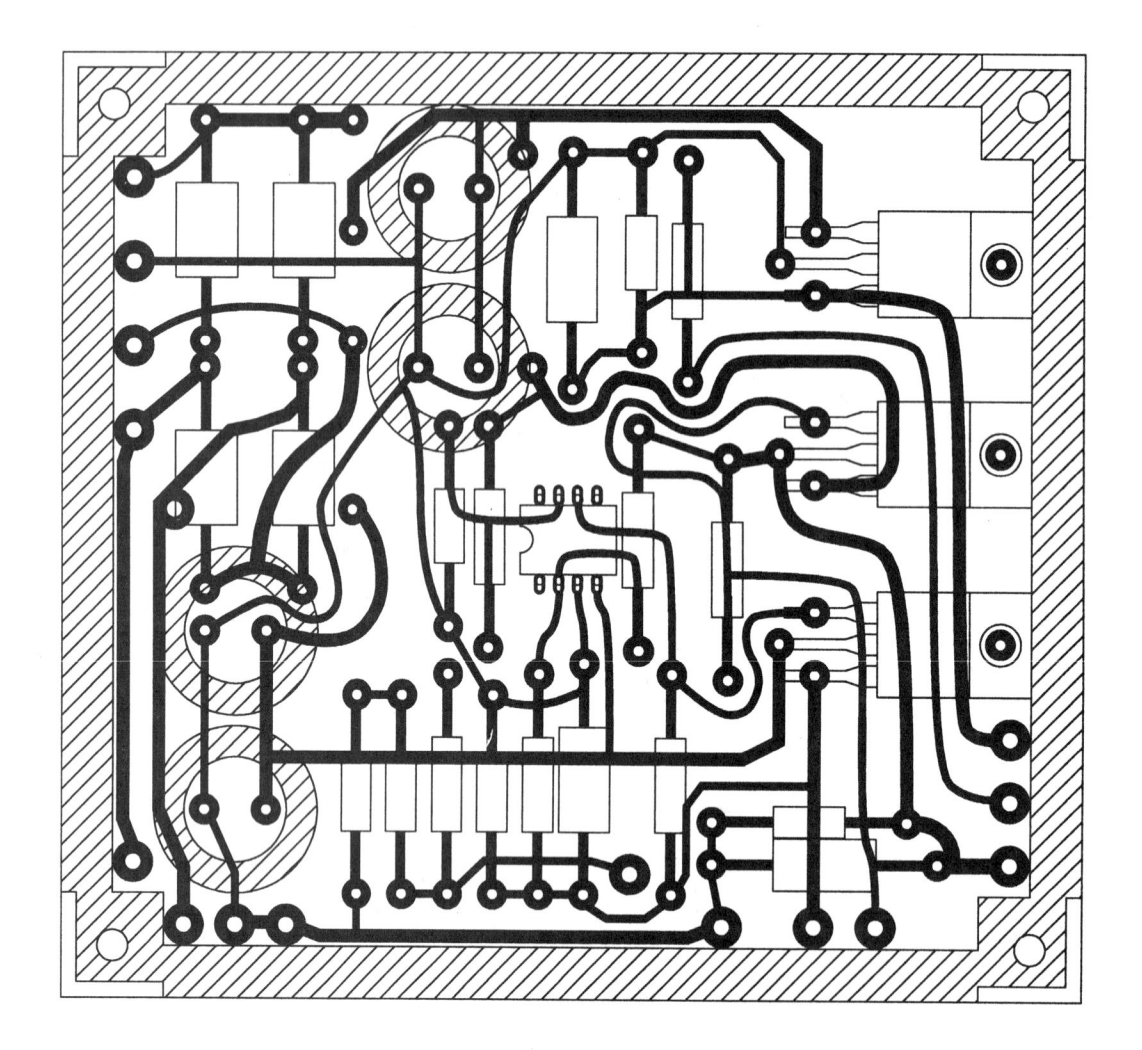

Figure 15.17 *Use a .75 mm PLINE to add the non-power conductors.*

10. Create the Artwork view as shown in figure 15.18. To create the Artwork view, turn off all layers except the trace and IC pad layers. Use the MIRROR command, selecting all visible objects in the Component view. Add the necessary text to the drawing.

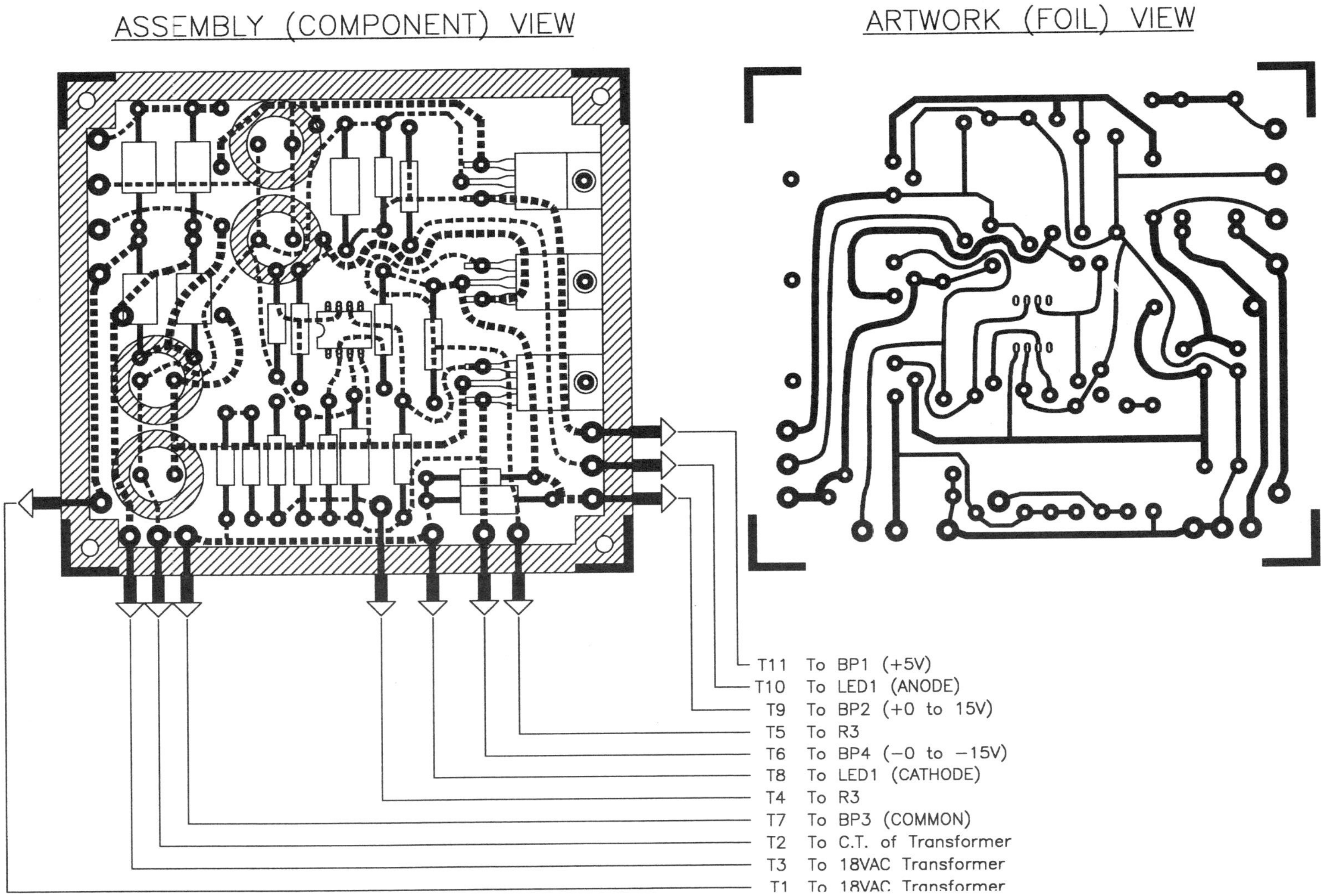

Figure 15.18 Create the Artwork view using the *MIRROR* command.

Unit 16: Creating Isometric Drawings

Overview

Isometric drawings are not very common in electronic drafting. If an electronic draftsman needs to create an isometric it is usually in cooperation with a mechanical draftsman or as part of a team. The isometric drawing may be of the housing for the electronic components. This drawing may be used in marketing, assembly, service manuals, or for consumer instruction manuals. When isometric drawings are created their inclusion to a complete detail or working drawing can greatly increase the understanding of the drawing. This unit will introduce the use of isometrics for mechanical detail drawings and mechanical isometric exploded assemblies.

Objectives

- Create isometric detail drawings.
- Create isometric exploded assembly drawings.

Introduction

When constructing multiview drawings, it is generally helpful to include a pictorial drawing to assist in the visualization of a part. As the main text presented, isometrics are just one of many different pictorial drawing types. Complete the Pictorial Drawing Types table 16.1 by filling in the blanks with the appropriate names of the pictorial drawing classifications and their types. Some blanks have already been filled to help begin this exercise.

			Isometric

Classification			
			General

		Perspective	

Table 16.1 *Pictorial Drawing Types.*

Because of their ease of creation, isometrics are used frequently in electronic drawing to ensure that a design is completely understood. In some situations, multiview drawings can seem like a "mish-mash" of visible lines, hidden lines, and centerlines. Without formal training it is difficult to visualize complicated multiview drawings. This is where the isometric can lend some assistance to the complete understanding of a design.

Section 1: Understanding Isometric and Pictorial Drawings

In drafting there are two popular types of pictorial drawings used to represent an object. They are the oblique and the isometric. Each of these is described in detail in the main text. Because isometrics are the most common, AutoCAD provides tools to assist in their creation such as:

- The isometric grid.
- The isometric snap.
- Isometric planes.

These tools allow the draftsperson to create accurate and stunning pictorial representations of objects that are to be prototyped or manufactured. There are two uses for isometric drawings: detail drawings and exploded assemblies.

> **FOR THE PROFESSIONAL**
>
> Isometrics are usually created full scale. Since there may not be room for an isometric drawing created at full scale on a multiview drawing, create the isometric drawing at full scale and then scale the drawing either 75% or 50% to ensure that it fits with the other views on the page.

Isometric Detail Drawings

An isometric detail drawing is simply a drawing of a single part. They are generally included to increase the visualization of a multiview drawing. It is important to note that they are not used for determining sizes and locations of features, so no dimensions or centerlines are placed on the drawing. Likewise, they should not be used for manufacturing. Their scale is not important since they are used for visualization only. What is important is that they complement the multiview with which they are grouped. Figure 16.1 displays a multiview drawing with a complementing isometric drawing in the upper right corner of the detail drawing.

The isometric in figure 16.1 was originally created at full scale but, since there was limited space, it was scaled down to 75%. This allowed it to fit in the area available. Notice the layout as well. The top and right extents of the drawing do not protrude past the top of the plan view and the right edge of the right-side view. The orientation of the isometric is in the most descriptive view.

> **SKILL BUILDER**
>
> To make their construction easy, create isometrics at full scale. Then scale the drawing either 75% or 50% to ensure that it fits with the other views on the page.

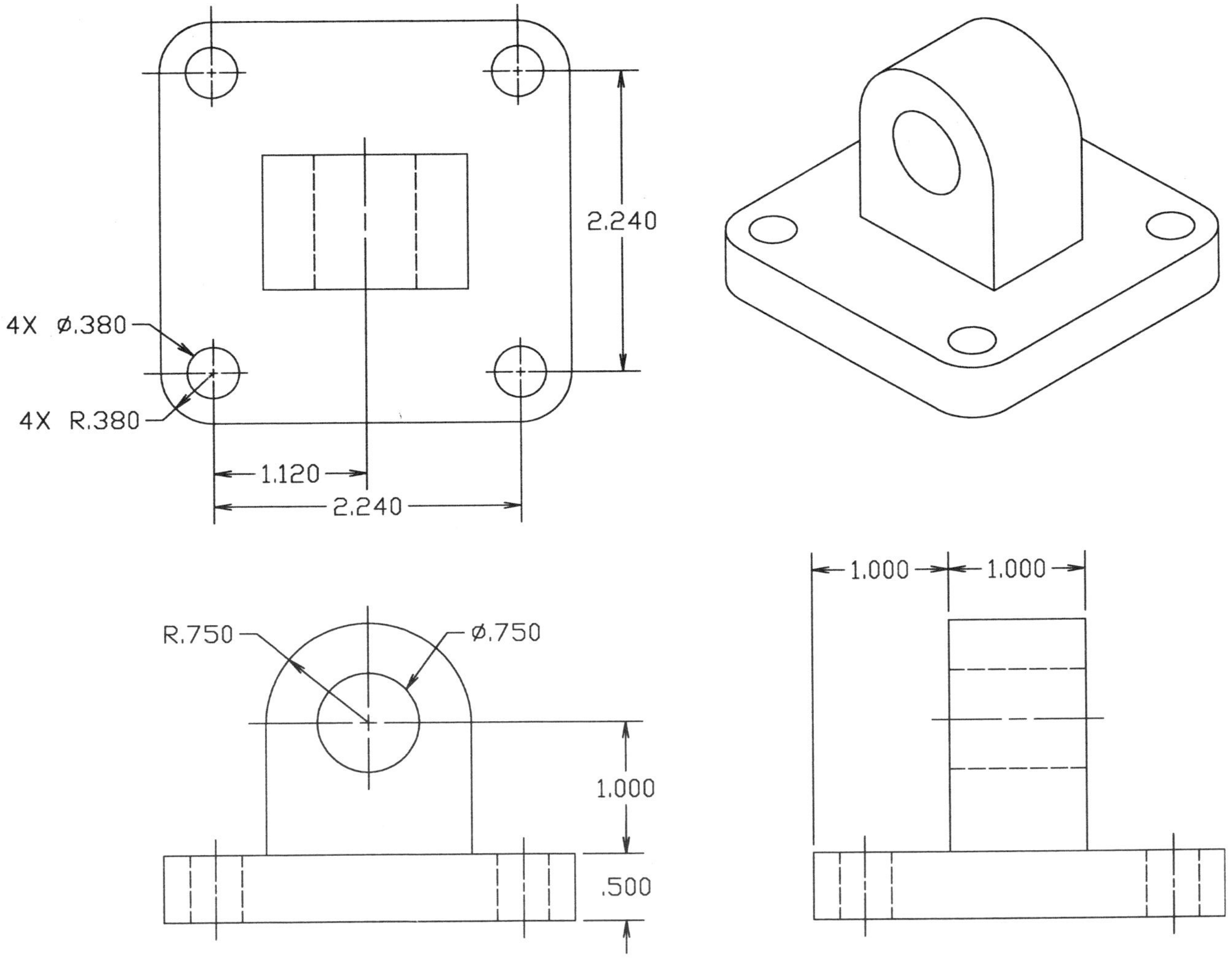

Figure 16.1 *This multiview drawing contains an isometric drawing.*

165

Isometric Exploded Assembly Drawings

In addition to isometric drawings of individual detail drawings, isometric drawings are also used to create exploded assembly drawings. Exploded assembly drawings are used to show the relationship between mating parts of an assembly. While any type of pictorial drawing may be used to create an exploded assembly, isometrics are the most common because of their ease of construction. While they may be time consuming to create, they can benefit more than one department in an organization. Isometric exploded assembly drawings may be found on working drawings, assembly instructions, and in sales brochures. A sample isometric exploded assembly is found in figure 16.2.

Notice in figure 16.2 that the relationship of the parts is enhanced by the use of centerlines. These centerlines visually indicate how the mating parts will be joined.

> **FOR THE PROFESSIONAL**
>
> Assembly drawings are not always exploded and they are not always isometrics. Consult an engineering drawing book for more information on other forms of assembly drawings.

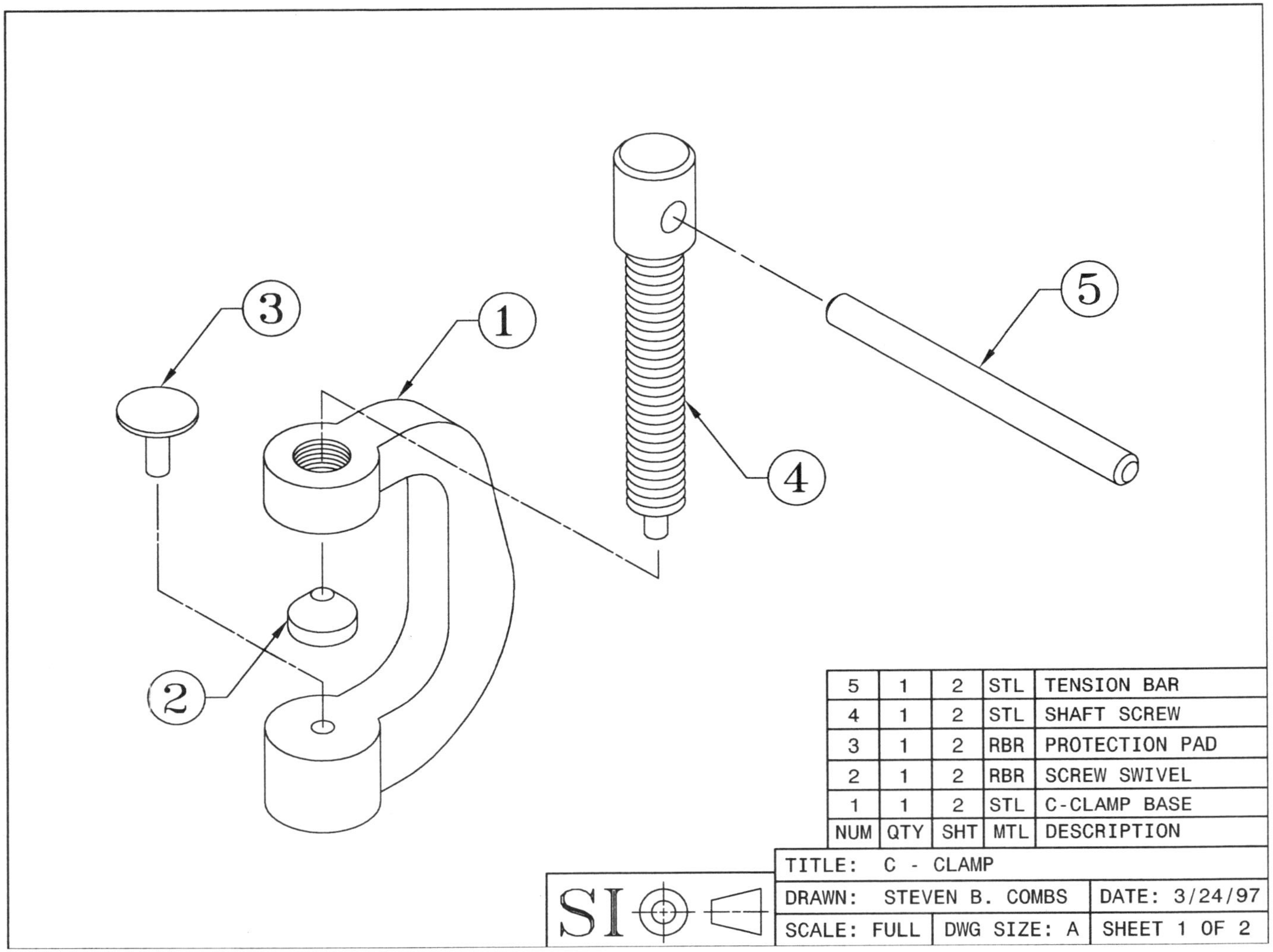

Figure 16.2 *An isometric exploded assembly of a C-clamp.*

Name _____

Unit 16 Review

List the three types of axonometric drawings.

1. _____

2. _____

3. _____

4. The _____ drawing is the most common type of axonometric created in electronic drafting.

5. _____ and _____ are typically not included on an isometric drawing.

6. An _____ _____ _____ is used to show the relationship between mating parts on a set of working drawings.

7. _____ drawings describe a single part or object.

8. _____ drawings describe an assembly of parts in a system.

9. True or False. Isometric drawings are always used to create exploded assembly drawings.

10. True or False. It is absolutely important to know the scale of an isometric drawing.

Unit 16 Assignment #1

In this assignment you will create an isometric drawing of the Clamp Stop drawing shown in figure 16.3. You are not to re-create the detail drawings, just create the isometric drawing by itself on a single sheet of paper. This assignment requires that you:

1. Determine the correct paper size.
2. Scale the drawing appropriately to ensure a balanced appearance on the page.
3. Add your name or a title block to the drawing.
4. Specify a name for the drawing file.
5. Correctly utilize isoplanes.
6. Correctly align ellipses.
7. Plot the drawing at an appropriate scale.

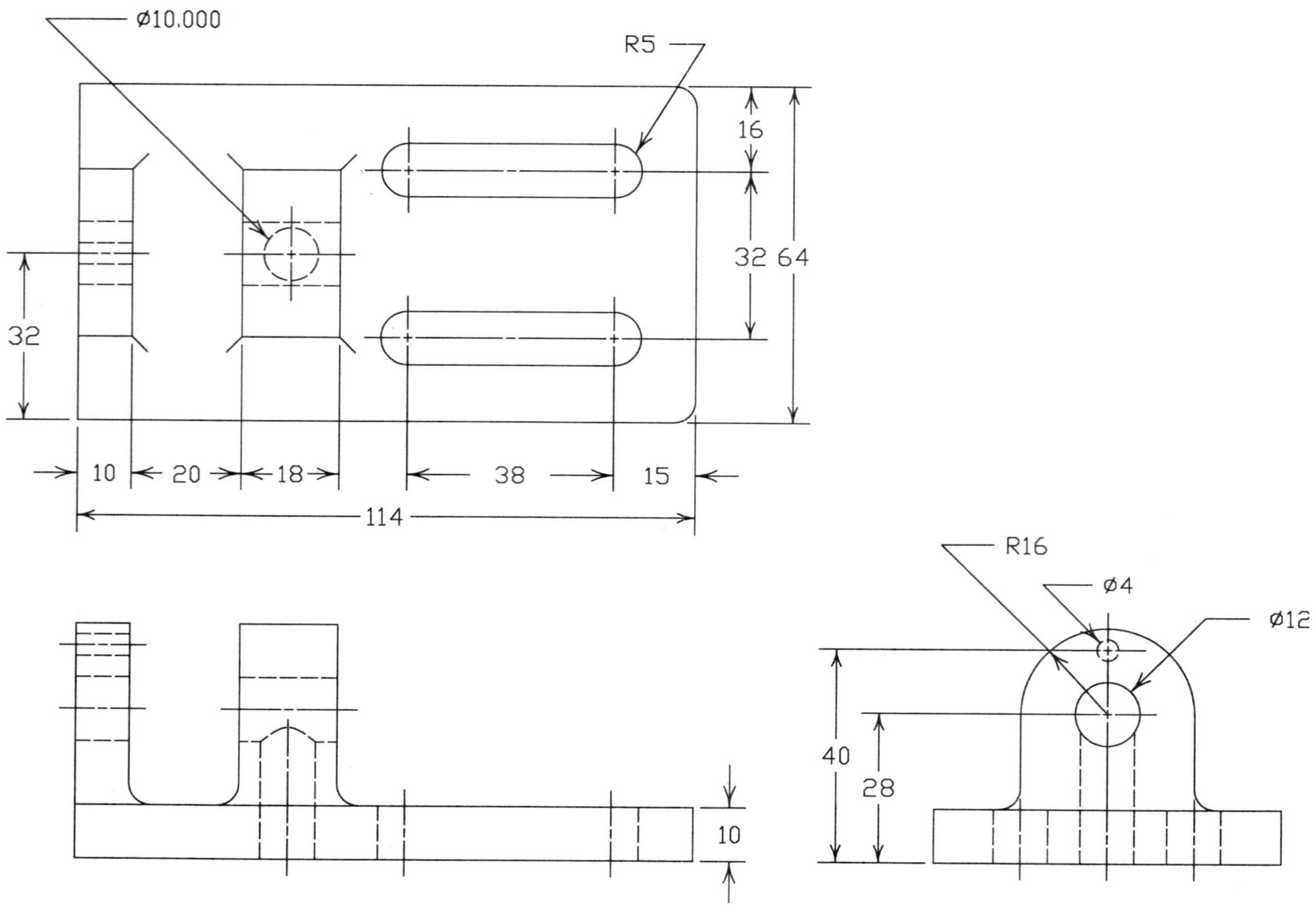

Figure 16.3 *The Clamp Stop assembly drawing.*

Unit 16 Assignment #2

In this assignment you will re-create the set of working drawings found in figures 16.4 and 16.5. Use the following directions to assist you in the creation of these drawings.

1. Create a new drawing named *C-Clamp Assembly.dwg*.

2. Create the exploded assembly found on the following pages. Use the dimensions from the C-Clamp drawing (also included on the following pages).

3. Create leaders with balloons to label all parts. Measurements for these balloons or any others needed may be taken from the drawing on the following page.

4. Create the title block and border as shown on the exploded assembly and make the appropriate annotations to the blocks.

5. Create the bill of materials.

6. Add the SI symbol as shown.

7. Save and plot the drawing.

8. Load the C-Clamp drawing you created previously in Unit 13. If you have not completed this assignment, create the detail drawings found in Figure 16.5.

9. Add balloons, the border, and the title block.

10. Move the detail drawings until a well-balanced drawing is created.

11. Save and plot the drawing.

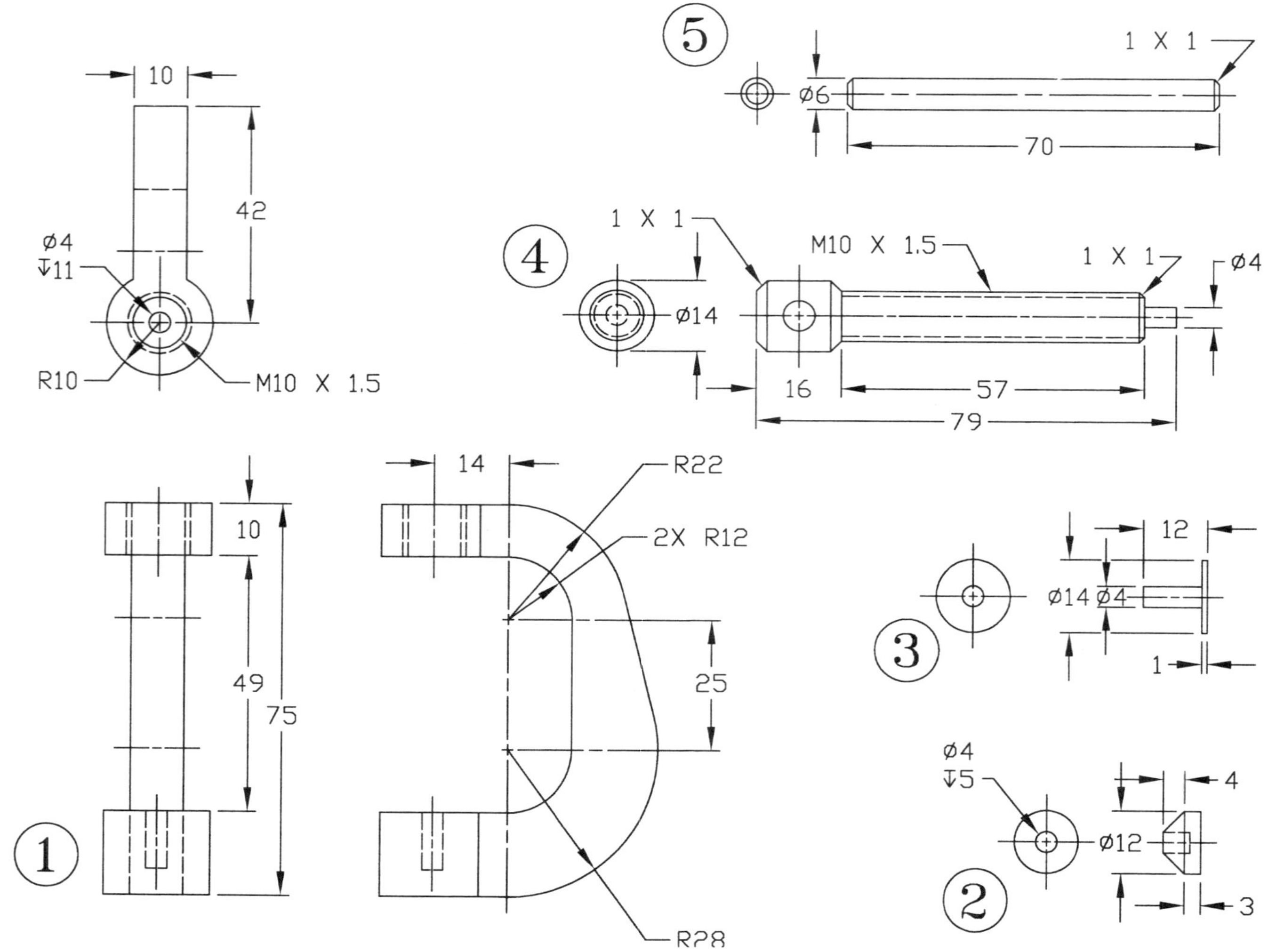

Figure 16.4 Sheet one of the C-Clamp assembly drawing.

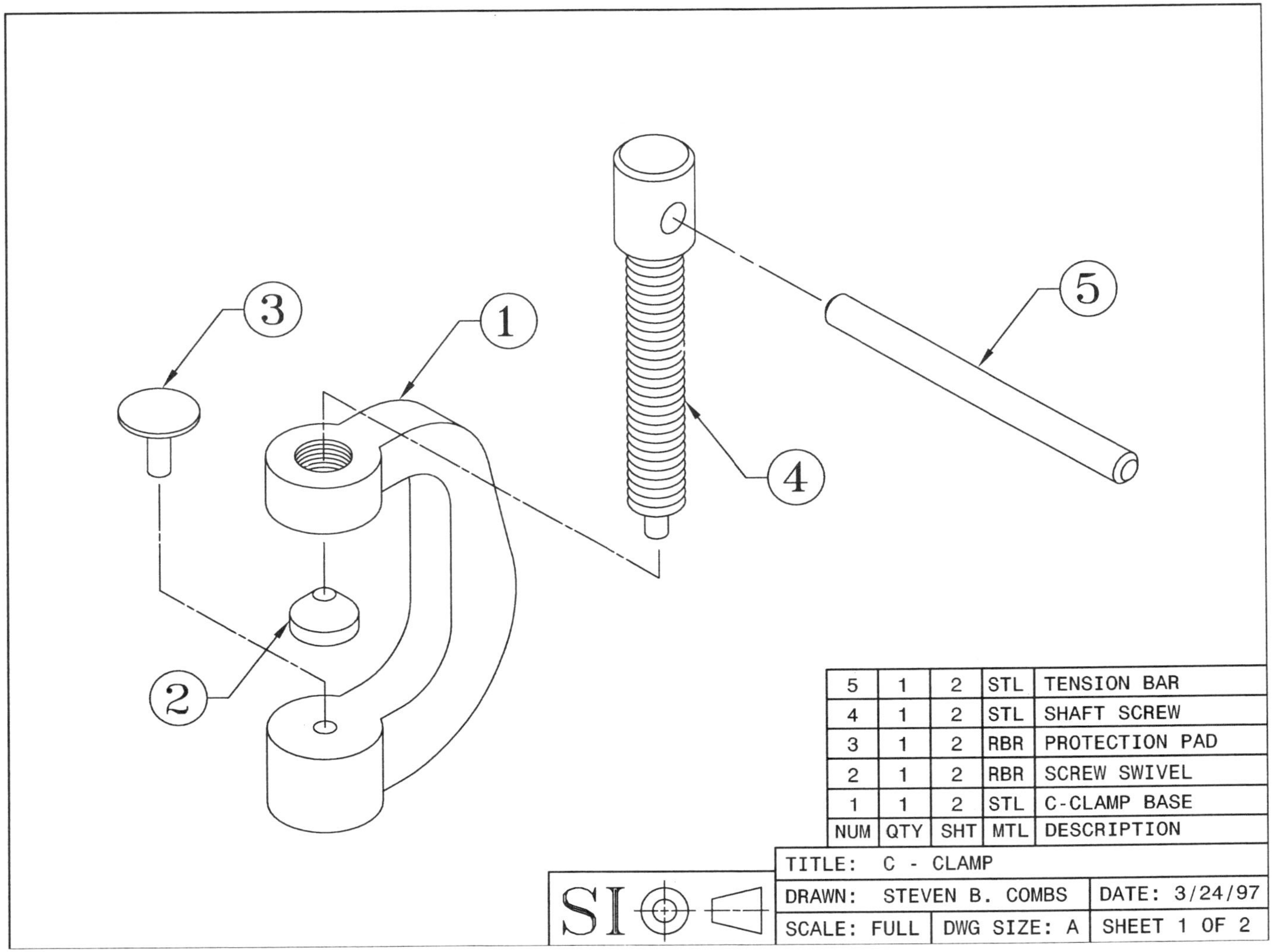

Figure 16.5 *Sheet two of the C-Clamp assembly drawing.*